LIBERTY IN E.........

1934-1994

LIBERTY IN BRITAIN
1934-1994

A Diamond Jubilee history of the
National Council for Civil Liberties

by
Brian Dyson

Civil Liberties Trust
1994

Civil Liberties Trust 1994

© Civil Liberties Trust
21 Tabard Street
London SE1 4LA
Telephone 071-403 3888

A CIP catalogue record for this book is available from the British Library.

The views expressed in this report are the author's and are not necessarily those of either the Civil Liberties Trust or Liberty (National Council for Civil Liberties).

ISBN 0900137 39 8

Designed and typeset by The Bears Communications, London (071-272 8760)
Printed by Crowes of Norwich (0603-403349)

Contents

Foreword

Liberty is now 60 years old – an important milestone in a proud history. From small beginnings, at a meeting in the Crypt of St Martin-in-the-Fields in 1934, Liberty has grown to be a significant, well-respected national organisation with thousands of members – an organisation which acts as a watchdog for our civil liberties, campaigns for change, undertakes test cases and provides authoritative briefing material and information.

It has had its ups and downs over the years, as this book makes clear. As governments and society have changed, and as the political climate has shifted, so have the campaigns which Liberty has had to initiate and lead. Often it has risen to the challenge, sometimes it has fallen short of what it hoped to achieve. At times it has been very hard to keep the flame of civil liberties alive – particularly in our political system where governments can so easily erode people's rights simply by passing new laws or issuing decrees.

But Liberty is proud that it has never bowed to government pressure and has always maintained an independent voice, consistently opposing abuses of civil liberties and human rights throughout its existence. Few other organisations could say the same about a 60-year period in which human rights and civil liberties have been attacked time after time. Therefore, in a way it is sad that we are still as busy as ever in 1994 defending many of these important rights, from the right of silence to the right of protest and freedom of movement.

That's why Liberty now believes we need to entrench rights as fundamental law in our society – we need a Bill of Rights in the UK to provide protection for *all* people against the power of government. But we must also place a greater emphasis on generating a popular culture of rights – it is not enough to communicate with policy makers and opinion formers, we have to make civil liberties and human rights the concerns of all people.

Our sister organisation, the American Civil Liberties Union, said in 1955 "Liberty is always unfinished business." It was right – we are unfinished business.

This history is just one chapter of a still unfolding story.

Andrew Puddephatt
General Secretary, Liberty

Preface

I am often asked, 'Why the University of Hull?' when the subject of the geo-
graphical location of the archives of the National Council for Civil Liberties
comes up. As a northerner myself, I am tempted to reply, 'And why not?'.
However, there is a more constructive answer.

Hull University Library – renamed the Brynmor Jones Library in 1970 –
began collecting the archives of leading pressure groups in the mid-1960s.
This was at the instigation of John Saville, of the University's Department of
Economic and Social History. He, along with the then University Librarian,
Philip Larkin, recognised the importance of pressure groups at a time when
few other repositories were interested. The Brynmor Jones Library's collection
of pressure group archives has subsequently grown to include the Union of
Democratic Control, the Co-operative Women's Guild (along with some of
the International CWG archives), the Socialist Medical (now Health) Association, the Joint Council for the Welfare of Immigrants, Justice, and the National
Council for Civil Liberties (now known as Liberty).

The importance of preserving the records of such bodies is achieving increasing recognition. Pressure groups have played a major role in many areas,
particularly those relating to the protection of individual and collective rights,
miscarriages of justice, and the observation of the activities of government.
This has applied especially during extended periods of one-party government, as has been the case in Britain in the 1930s, 1950s, 1980s and so far
in the 1990s. The NCCL archive, in particular, provides an important social,
political and legal record of Britain in the latter two-thirds of the twentieth
century. As a civil liberties collection, it is second to none in this country.
Philip Larkin took a personal interest in acquiring the collection for his library,
visiting the Council's offices twice during the negotiation, and leaving his
own mark in the archive in the form of 15 letters sent to NCCL staff between
1969 and 1970 when the first batch of records was transferred to Hull.

The collection now fills some 750 boxes, and is growing steadily. The
fascination of the NCCL archive is endless, with records of topics ranging
from anti-fascism in the 1930s, to the rights of servicemen in the 1940s, mental
health reform in the 1950s, race relations in the 1960s, women's rights in
the 1970s, miscarriages of justice in the 1980s, and the most recent campaigns
for a bill of rights and criminal justice reform in the 1990s. Of necessity, this
short history presents a curtailed view of the NCCL's activities at any one
time. The emphasis, as in all histories, is on great issues and great campaigns,
of which, in NCCL's case, there have been many. It is important to remember,

however, that throughout its life the main job of NCCL and its staff has been to help, support, and if necessary fight for, those thousands of individuals who have nowhere else to turn.

I am most grateful for the help and co-operation afforded to me by the staff of Liberty whilst preparing this book, and in particular by Matthew Brown, Chris Jones, Nettie Pollard, Andrew Puddephatt, Hilary Ransom, Marie Ryan, John Wadham and Jenny Watson. Valuable comments on earlier drafts have been freely provided by Malcolm Hurwitt, Rod Robertson, Sylvia Scaffardi, John Taylor and Peter Thornton QC. Colleagues in the Brynmor Jones Library who have also helped, sometimes unknowingly, include Christine Richardson, Helen Roberts and Jean Sushams, and the staff of the Photographic and Copy Service. Above all, I must thank my wife, Philippa, not least for tolerating yet another working Christmas.

Brian Dyson

May 1994
Brynmor Jones Library,
University of Hull.

The author

Brian Dyson was born in Bolton, Lancashire, in 1953. He has degrees in contemporary history/economics and international politics, and, unusually, is qualified both as an archivist and as a librarian. He is married and has lived in Hull since 1981. He became Hull University Archivist in 1987, and in this capacity is custodian of the archives of Liberty and other pressure groups. He is the author or editor of over 20 professional books and articles. He belongs to no political party and is not a member of Liberty.

Abbreviations used

BBC . . . . *British Broadcasting Corporation*
BJL . . . . . *Brynmor Jones Library, University of Hull*
BUF. . . . . *British Union of Fascists*
CCAF. . . . *Co-ordinating Committee Against Fascism*
CCL. . . . . *Council for Civil Liberties*
CLT . . . . . *Civil Liberties Trust*
CND . . . . *Campaign for Nuclear Disarmament*
CPGB . . . *Communist Party of Great Britain*
CWG. . . . *Co-operative Women's Guild*
DR . . . . . *Defence Regulation*
EC. . . . . . *Executive Committee*
ECHR . . . *European Convention on Human Rights*
GCHQ. . . *Government Communications Head Quarters, Cheltenham*
GLC. . . . . *Greater London Council*
IRA . . . . . *Irish Republican Army*
IS . . . . . . *International Socialists*
KC. . . . . . *King's Counsel*
LLL . . . . . *Law and Liberty League*
MEPO . . . *Metropolitan Police*
NCAC . . . *National Council Against Conscription*
NCL. . . . . *National Council of Labour*
NF. . . . . . *National Front*
NMA . . . . *Nottinghamshire Miners' Association*
NUJ. . . . . *National Union of Journalists*
NUM . . . . *National Union of Mineworkers*
NUWM . . *National Unemployed Workers' Movement*
PCLG. . . . *Parliamentary Civil Liberties Group*
PRO . . . . *Public Record Office*
RAE. . . . . *Royal Aircraft Establishment, Farnborough*
RASC. . . . *Royal Army Surgical Corps, Aldershot*
SCCL . . . . *Scottish Council for Civil Liberties*
TUC . . . . *Trades Union Congress*
UN . . . . . *United Nations*
UNESCO . *United Nations Educational, Scientific and Cultural Organisation*
WEA . . . . *Workers' Educational Association*

1 Ronald Kidd and the birth of the Council

When Ronald Kidd established the Council for Civil Liberties early in 1934 it was not the first modern organisation concerned with the defence of individual and collective freedoms in Great Britain. Nor was it the first body to bear that name, though some of the forerunners were more significant than others.

One of the most important was established in the 1880s. In late 1887 a series of meetings and demonstrations held in Trafalgar Square by the unemployed, Irish Home Rulers, and others, were dealt with by police using baton charges. This prompted William Morris, writing in the *Pall Mall Gazette*, to propose the establishment of a Law and Liberty League, which quickly attracted the support of other well-known campaigners, including Annie Besant, WT Stead and the Reverend Stewart Headlam. Its basic aim was to help those who had been unjustly arrested or imprisoned by the police. In the most serious incident of the time, on 13 November 1887, a demonstration in and around Trafalgar Square was brutally attacked by the police, leaving three dead, 200 or so in hospital and 75 protesters under arrest – this was the original 'Bloody Sunday'. William Morris was in the thick of the demonstration that day, as was George Bernard Shaw, who subsequently had the distinction of having been a member of the Law and Liberty League, the first National Council for Civil Liberties, and (from 1939) the second NCCL.

The Law and Liberty League did not survive very long, possibly because of its concentration on one main issue, namely personal freedom in relation to the police.[1] A similar fate befell the first NCCL, which began life in late 1915 as the National Council Against Conscription. The threat (and almost immediate imposition) of conscription was seen as a major infringement of liberties. However, in the autumn of 1916, the broader name was adopted, reflecting a general interest on the part of members in all matters affecting personal freedoms. Under both names, and in its various offices around London, the organisation appears to have enjoyed the close attention of the police authority acting under the Defence of the Realm Act, and reports in contemporary newspapers such as *The Times* are of police raids and the removal of incriminating publications and records.

For most of its existence, this first NCCL had an Advice Department, which assisted several thousand enquirers, and a Record Office, which gave information to speakers, writers and others on subjects within the Council's scope.

The two departments were merged immediately after the end of the War and it remained active at least until December 1918, when it issued a letter to prospective voters in the impending general election from its premises at Bedford House, 33 Henrietta Street, Covent Garden, London WC2. Its officers then were: WC Anderson MP (President); Dr John Clifford, JA Hobson, HW Massingham, Bertrand Russell and Robert Smillie (Vice-Presidents); Mrs Philip Snowden (Treasurer); and BN Langdon-Davies (Secretary). This first NCCL does not appear to have survived long after the annual meeting of February 1919. In truth, for most if not all of its existence, it seems to have been completely over-shadowed by other 'peace' organisations, such as the Union of Democratic Control and the No-Conscription Fellowship.[2]

Hunger marches and the use of police *agents provocateurs*

The early 1930s was a time of massive unemployment, cuts in public relief, and stringent means testing. It was also a period of organised protest, manifest most publicly in the famous hunger marches. The first major hunger march reached London on 1 November 1932 with a petition containing one million signatures protesting against a 10 per cent cut in unemployment benefit and the means test imposed in November 1931. The march was organised by the Communist-led National Unemployed Workers' Movement, whose leader Wal Hannington was promptly arrested. The petition was confiscated by the police, who also used *agents provocateurs* disguised as working men to incite the marchers assembled in Trafalgar Square to violence. This activity was observed by Ronald Kidd.

Ronald Hubert Kidd was born in 1889 and brought up in Hampstead. He had entered University College London as a science student but did not take his degree. As a young man he campaigned in the women's suffrage movement and lectured for the Workers' Educational Association and other groups before going into service during the first world war. Discharged on the grounds of poor health, he was briefly secretary to the Wellcome Historical Medical Museum, before joining the Civil Service – at first with the Ministry of Labour, where he edited a daily bulletin and then a weekly gazette, and later with the Ministry of Pensions. After resigning in disgust at the cuts in pensions for shell-shocked war veterans, he freelanced in journalism, advertising and public relations, making some of the many contacts which were later to be of considerable use to the fledgling NCCL. He acted on the stage, and even took small parts in films. For a period he became an actor-manager for tours of London productions, a time when he met the young Sylvia Crowther-Smith (later Scaffardi) – 15 years his junior – who became his companion.

Kidd's estranged wife and child lived in Bristol, where he had at one time been stage and scenic director of the Little Theatre. Whilst Crowther-Smith worked as a freelance editor, Kidd ventured next into publishing, and then into bookselling and, at the time of the arrival of the first hunger march, was employed running the tiny Punch & Judy bookshop in Villiers Street, off the Strand, where he specialised in radical and left-wing titles. Crowther-Smith later described him in her memoir of the period as a 'very individual brotherhood-of-man type' of socialist, who never joined any political party.[3] Another early associate, Claud Cockburn, writing for *Punch* in February 1955, recalled that Kidd was a 'saint-like man ... who looked like the canon of some rather forward-looking diocese...'[4]

It is worth noting that Kidd was by no means alone in his concern for the defence of liberty. Others had taken initiatives. The Bristol Council for the Defence of Civil Liberties, for example, was established in April 1933. At the national level, however, there remained a need for leadership by a well-known figure of stature. Though Kidd never regarded himself as such a man, 1933 did see his elevation to celebrity status of a sort.

On 5 August 1933 an article by AP Herbert in *Week-End Review* (later incorporated into Kingsley Martin's *New Statesman and Nation*) discussed the use of police *agents provocateurs* against after-hours drinkers in public houses and night clubs. Kidd initiated a series of exchanges with Herbert in *Week-End Review* and shifted the debate to the use of such agents against the hunger marchers. Eventually Herbert offered to go with Gerald Barry (editor of *Week-End Review*) to visit the Commissioner of the Metropolitan Police, Lord Trenchard, to demand a public inquiry. They were armed for the visit with sworn affadavits presented by Kidd and Douglas Jefferies (a member of the NUWM and the Communist Party of Great Britain) concerning police tactics during the hunger march of 1932. Trenchard denied that there was any need for an inquiry. But Kidd had made his point and, in the 28 October issue of the *Review*, in an article entitled 'Mr Kidd and the Agent-Provocateur', Herbert warmly praised him for his public spirit in raising the whole issue.[5]

On 17 December 1933, Kidd and Crowther-Smith were present during an anti-Nazi demonstration in Trafalgar Square, organised by a group called International Labour Defence, when two men were arrested for using 'insulting words and behaviour'. Kidd and Crowther-Smith made voluntary written statements alleging that the police had used excessive force during the demonstration. Kidd expected to be called as a witness at the trial later that week but was not. A (typically biased) police superintendent commenting on the case minuted: 'I look upon Mr Kidd as an impossible man, not at all particular as to the truth. He endeavours to create the impression that he is acting in a public sprited manner, but I am of the opinion that he is affected by political bias and an obvious dislike for the police and probably anything that stands for law and order.' Kidd sent a formal letter of complaint to the Home Secretary on 26 December, to no effect.[6] Clearly, someone or something with more influence was needed.

The next (and largest) hunger march of this period, again organised by the National Unemployed Workers' Movement, was due to rally in London on Sunday 25 February 1934. The Home Secretary, Sir John Gilmour, primed the public by giving dire warnings of serious disorder and calling for people to be careful when the marchers arrived. The police prepared the ground in their own way by arresting the Communist Party leaders, Harry Pollitt and Tom Mann, just two days before and charging them with sedition – charges later thrown out at their trial in July. Kidd, fearing the repeated use of *agents provocateurs* in an attempt to incite the hunger marchers, decided to take the initiative.

Unfortunately, a combination of circumstances, including Sylvia Crowther-Smith's absence at this time following a death in her family, the loss of most of the early records (including the first minute books) and Kidd's own early death, mean that knowledge of this first phase of the NCCL's existence is rather sketchy. It would seem, however, that Kidd made his first moves some time in January 1934. Indeed, an advertisement in the *New Statesman* of 3 November 1934 referred to the Council for Civil Liberties as having been set up 'in January last as a permanent non-party body to resist all encroachments on our liberties'.

The result of Kidd's actions was the establishment of a provisional committee with representatives from literature, art, journalism, medicine and the law. A circular letter headed 'The Council for Civil Liberties' and dated 1 February 1934 drew immediate support from Kingsley Martin, Henry Nevinson, Dr Edith Summerskill and Professor Lascelles Abercrombie.[7] The inaugural meeting of the Council was held at St Martin-in-the-Fields Vestry Hall (lent by the Reverend 'Dick' Shepherd, a member of the first Executive Committee and also one of the first Vice-Presidents) at 8pm on 22 February 1934. Fewer than 20 people were present, all by invitation. The topics discussed included the general policy of the Council; the nature and aim of the hunger march; the rights of free speech and assembly; police provocation and irregularities; and fascist tendencies in Britain.[8]

An Executive Committee was elected, as follows:

Ambrose Appelbe. . . . . (Solicitor)
GHC Bing . . . . (Barrister)
Vera Brittain. . . . . (Author)
Claud Cockburn . . . . (Journalist)
Dudley Collard. . . . . (Barrister)
Sylvia Crowther-Smith. . . . . (Honorary Treasurer)
David Freeman. . . . . (Solicitor)
R Shepherd . . . . (Editor of *Free Speech & Assembly Bulletin*)
J Pascoe. . . . . (Likewise)
Douglas Goldring. . . . . (Author)
Mrs C Haden Guest. . . . . (Author)
Professor Harold Laski . . . . (Academic)
Kingsley Martin. . . . . (Journalist/Editor)
Mrs Evelyn Sharp Nevinson. . . . . (Author)
Llewellyn Rees . . . . (General Secretary of Equity)
Dr Edith Summerskill . . . . (County Councillor)
Alun Thomas . . . . (International Labour Defence)
Mrs Amabel Williams-Ellis. . . . . (Author)

The Committee was empowered to co-opt, and shortly afterwards added:

Trevor Blewitt . . . . (Civil Liberties Press Panel)
Professor GEG Catlin . . . . . (Academic, and husband of Vera Brittain)
Dr Ivor Jennings. . . . . (Academic)
Dr Jeffrey Samuel . . . . (Academic)
WH Thompson. . . . . (Solicitor)
ES Watkins. . . . . (Solicitor)

The founding meeting also reached agreement on a public statement to be made on the situation. This took the form of a letter in *The Manchester Guardian* on 24 February 1934 headed 'Hunger-Marchers in London', and signed by 14 of the more prominent members, including Clement Attlee, Vera Brittain, AP Herbert, Harold Laski, Kingsley Martin, DN Pritt, Edith Summerskill, HG Wells and the Secretary, Ronald Kidd. The letter expressed apprehension about the imminent arrival of the hunger marchers and the likely behaviour of the police towards them. It continued:

In view of the general and alarming tendency to encroachment on the liberty of the citizen, there has recently been formed a Council for Civil Liberties. One of the special duties of this Council will be to maintain a vigilant observation of the proceedings of the next few days. Relevant and well-authenticated reports by responsible persons will be welcomed and investigated by the Council.

The promised 'vigilant observation' of the arrival of the hunger marchers took the form of observers in Hyde Park on 25 February, including such luminaries as HG Wells, Julian Huxley, Harold Laski, Henry Nevinson, Winifred Holtby and Vera Brittain. In the event, the demonstration by over 15,000 people, with about 5,000 police in attendance, was entirely peaceful. Although the Prime Minister, Ramsay MacDonald, refused to meet a delegation of marchers, the 10 per cent cut in unemployment relief was rescinded in the annual Budget speech a few weeks later. Writing his first *Annual Report* for the Council in 1935, Kidd commented: 'Experience has shown that the presence of responsible observers, who are prepared to go into the witness-box, has a wholesome influence.'[9] This lesson was not forgotten.

The organisation

The Council was renamed the National Council for Civil Liberties (NCCL) in November 1934. The writer, EM Forster, was elected President when the first choice, the distinguished liberal journalist, war correspondent and writer, Henry Nevinson, declined on grounds of age and ill-health. Ironically, illness later forced Forster to step down as President in 1936, when he was replaced by the 80-year-old Nevinson. By the end of 1934 some 51 Vice-Presidents had been acquired, plus two for Northern Ireland. The list of distinguished names – always displayed prominently on the NCCL's letter paper, press releases and so on – included: Clement Attlee, Aneurin Bevan, Vera Brittain, GDH Cole, Havelock Ellis, Dingle Foot, Victor Gollancz, GP Gooch, AP Herbert, Winifred Holtby, Julian Huxley, CEM Joad, George Lansbury, Harold Laski, David Low, Kingsley Martin, AA Milne, Henry W Nevinson, FW Pethick-Lawrence, Lord Ponsonby, JB Priestley, DN Pritt, Bertrand Russell, RH Tawney, HG Wells and Rebecca West.

Nevertheless, in its early years the NCCL was effectively run by Ronald Kidd with the assistance of Sylvia Crowther-Smith. The first known address was 43 Villiers Street, London WC2, given in the letter to *The Manchester Guardian* on 24 February 1934. This was in fact the address of Kidd's 'Punch

& Judy' bookshop, which was later described by Crowther-Smith as 'a cubby hole next door to the lift in Embankment Chambers'.[10] A circular letter sent out to prospective Vice-Presidents, dated 15 March 1934, had the same address at its head.[11] This appears to have been used as a holding address only.

In reality, until April 1935, operations were directed from 3 Dansey Place (formerly Dansey Yard), Shaftesbury Avenue, W1, which is where Kidd and Crowther-Smith were living. Kidd described it in his first *Annual Report* as 'an obscure office which, although situated in the West End, was extremely difficult to find'.[12] Crowther-Smith remembered the address as 'an ugly little open-ended cobbled mews, jammed right behind Shaftesbury Avenue and serving as a passageway between Wardour Street and Macclesfield Street'.[13] A set of steep, metal stairs led to a single, bare-boarded room, half of which was partitioned off as living quarters. The office enjoyed views over an adjacent (and thankfully disused) public urinal. Claud Cockburn recalled 'a hovel-like dwelling opposite a public convenience in a mews...'[14] This was not all – Kingsley Martin, another early participant, remembered that 'Close by was the base from which all the sandwich-board men in London, or so it seemed, passed in and out on their peripatetic profession.'[15] To complicate matters still further, the rest of the building was occupied by the London Provincial Films Motor Transport Company Limited.[16]

Initially the NCCL paid Kidd rent for this accommodation, before moving to the more traditional practice of paying him a small salary. Crowther-Smith became paid Assistant Secretary in late July 1934 and a part-time clerk was employed later in the year, whilst hourly-paid 'temps' were taken on as necessary. All concerned must have found the conditions very trying, particularly Kidd whom, Cockburn thought, 'liked order, and was surrounded by something awfully like chaos'.[17]

The successes of the NCCL's first year were achieved with this very small staff and a total budget of £946 0s. 6d. There was a nominal subscription fee of five shillings for individuals but even by 1936 membership had reached only about 1,300. Of greater importance was the help given to Kidd by the Executive Committee, which met monthly in a hired hotel room in nearby Craven Street, whilst a General Purposes Sub-Committee met weekly to deal with more urgent matters. Considerable help was received from a number of brilliant barristers on this Committee, including DN Pritt and Dudley Collard, who frequently took up civil liberty cases without claimimg expenses. Both Committees were chaired by WH Thompson, an efficient and very successful solicitor of the radical left, whose role in the early years of the NCCL has largely been neglected. Crowther-Smith later described him as 'a tough Lancastrian, a big personable man with a large presence, a genial manner, the successful single boss of a lucrative solicitor's firm that specialised in the industrial field and had a thriving trade union practice.'[18] Forster also regularly attended Executive Committee meetings, although he apparently said little, preferring to put his thoughts in writing to Kidd afterwards. His fame, and that of the NCCL's Vice-Presidents and associates, were what mattered as far as Kidd was concerned.

2 From strength to strength: the 1930s

The Council was later to become known for its support of individuals – both legal and otherwise – and there are many celebrated cases in its files. However, the main characteristic of the NCCL during its early years was its role as a national campaigning organisation and this has continued to the present day. A series of campaigns, notably in the 1930s and 1950s, and again in the 1980s and 1990s, have played a crucial role in its success. The first of these began almost immediately after its formation.

The Incitement to Disaffection Bill

Sedition had long played on the minds of successive governments. But it was the Invergordon 'Mutiny' of September 1931 which convinced the Government and military authorities of the need to shield members of the armed forces from all forms of what were viewed as potentially seductive political influences. The Bill put forward to do this, in 1934, effectively prevented members of the armed forces from encountering *any* influences at all. This Bill also presented the NCCL with the campaign which effectively ensured its continuation after its early success with the hunger marches. It moved swiftly to organise public protest against the Incitement to Disaffection (or 'Sedition') Bill which made it a criminal offence to 'maliciously and advisedly ... seduce any member of His Majesty's Forces from his duty or allegiance' or possess any 'documents of such a nature that the dissemination of copies thereof among members of His Majesty's Forces would constitute such an offence'. An NCCL leaflet explained that 'The Bill makes it a criminal offence to possess any document of such a character that, if it were distributed among the armed forces of the Crown, might tend to seduce them from their allegiance. All pacifist and anti-war literature obviously falls into this category. It would become dangerous to possess such literature.'[19]

The wide-ranging campaign involved an emergency delegate conference held jointly with the London Trades Council in the Memorial Hall London on 9 June 1934, national and local meetings and conferences, mass demonstrations in Trafalgar Square (again jointly with the London Trades Council) and public debates. Kidd drew upon the legal advice of people like Pritt, who made detailed analyses of the Government's proposals. Correspondence on the subject between Kidd and Sir Thomas Inskip, the Attorney General, became rather heated, both in public and private. Kidd accused Inskip of misinforming the House of Commons about the purpose of the Bill (letter in *The Spectator*, 6 July 1934) and before agreeing to meet a deputation from the Council, Inskip demanded (and received) a public retraction in *The Spectator*.[20] This delegation, led by Forster, eventually met Inskip on 30 July, but to little obvious effect. The high point of the campaign was a mock trial held on 6 November at the Friends' Meeting House, Euston Road, featuring David Low (the famous cartoonist), Miles Malleson, Kingsley Martin and WH Thompson, which involved Low being charged with producing a cartoon which seduced a member of the armed forces (played by Kingsley Martin).

Forster found the public disagreement between Inskip and Kidd rather unpleasant, particularly as he was on record as having described Inskip as 'reliable', whereas Kidd had publicly questioned Inskip's veracity. Forster was equally unhappy about a further aspect of the campaign, which involved members of NCCL pledging themselves to go to the military establishment at Aldershot and distribute copies of allegedly 'seditious' literature should the Sedition Bill become law. Over-reacting to what was really intended as a ploy, Forster wrote to Kidd on 6 October offering to resign if this 'pledge' was made compulsory.[21] The resignation was not accepted and Forster actually appeared and spoke at a public meeting on the subject held on 18 October, but gently made his point by not taking the chair.

The Bill duly became law in November, albeit after considerable modification, and the highly unpopular Act has since seldom been used in practice. Indeed, its first major use was in December 1975, when 14 members of the British Withdrawal from Northern Ireland Movement were accused of conspiring to incite soldiers to desert and of being in possession of seditious leaflets. Some of those charged were represented by the NCCL and their acquittal was a notable success.[22]

Censorship: Non-flam films

Another issue of much concern was the misuse by local authorities of the Cinematograph Act of 1909, which had been intended to preserve public safety by empowering the authorities to issue licences for suitable establishments. In practice, the authorities started refusing licences to those exhibiting films of which they disapproved – usually on the basis of sexual or political content. The film industry tried to solve the problem by self-regulation and set up the British Board of Film Censors in 1912. However, banned films (such as Eisenstein's *Battleship Potemkin*) could still be seen in small clubs and colleges where exhibitors used miniature cellulose acetate or 'non-flammable' copies.

In 1934 the Home Office announced its intention of extending the 1909 controls to include these non-flam films, ostensibly in the interests of public safety. The NCCL produced a pamphlet arguing against this, and fought a well-publicised test case. The Home Office attempted to obtain a judicial ruling on inflammability during the trial of 11 men from Bolden Colliery Miners' Lodge following their summons to Jarrow Police Court for showing a miniature non-flam film in the Miners' Hall. Much to the surprise of those in court, and the men from the Home Office, the miners were represented by WH Thompson, with financial backing from the British Institute of Adult Education. Thompson and his technical experts demonstrated the effects of fire on the various types of film, proving that the cellulose acetate of the miniature film would not burn. The case was dismissed and costs were charged to the police in what was another significant victory for the Council.

The Home Office eventually abandoned its plans in 1938. However, a further (unsuccessful) attempt was made in 1952, and for many years the Council's *Annual Report* and newsletters called for continued vigilance in this area.

Northern Ireland

Since its political separation from the rest of Ireland in 1922, the legal and policing systems of the province of Northern Ireland have been characterised by the denial of basic human rights. Under the Special Powers Acts of 1922 and 1933 *habeas corpus* had effectively been suspended; arrests could be made on suspicion and there was detention and internment without trial. At the suggestion of Geoffrey Bing KC, a member of the Executive Committee, the NCCL decided in late 1934 to investigate the operation of these Acts.

A Commission of Inquiry was established in January 1935, chaired by Aylmer Digby KC, with Margery Fry (principal of Somerville College, 1926-31), William McKeag (a Liberal MP and solicitor) and EL Mallalieu (a Liberal MP and a barrister). Kidd himself visited 20 towns in the province and was shocked by what he found, particularly when he witnessed a major outbreak of sectarian rioting in Belfast in June 1935. The findings of the Commission were delayed when Digby unfortunately fell ill and died, although he had approved the final draft of its report published in 1936.[23] This supposedly 'emergency' legislation was condemned for bringing the law into disrepute and driving the Government's opponents into the arms of extremists. The report was highly critical of the authoritarian system of government operating in the province.

Its publication was widely covered and well received in the press and succeeded in upsetting the Northern Ireland Government. For example, a draft of a letter written on behalf of the NCCL by Harold Laski in July 1936 protests in defence of three professors at Queen's University, Belfast, whom the Unionist MP, William Grant, had suggested ought to be disciplined for their connection with NCCL and for their failure to contradict the Northern Ireland report.[24] This both typifies the problem of official reactions to the NCCL and, coincidentally, again shows how Kidd was able to call upon distinguished individuals to assist in drafting reports and letters.

The report represented the start of the NCCL's long interest in Northern Ireland, one which has continued to the present day. It was reprinted in 1972, a time when its conclusions still appeared to be highly relevant.

Duncan v. Jones: the first major individual case

During the great campaign concerning the Incitement to Disaffection Bill there arose an individual case which is now considered a landmark in the law on public order, even though it was lost. It was the first of many such cases taken up by NCCL.

On 30 July 1934 Mrs Kath Duncan, a member of the National Unemployed Workers' Movement, was trying to speak about the Sedition Bill to a small crowd outside a training centre for the unemployed in a cul-de-sac in Deptford. She was ordered by a police officer to move further down the road, refused, and was arrested and charged with obstructing an officer in the execution of his duty. She was fined £2 plus five guineas costs. NCCL recognised that there were important principles at stake, particularly the fact that obstructing an officer in the course of his duty had previously been confined to physical interference only. It supported Mrs Duncan's appeal to Quarter Sessions and provided two lawyers (DN Pritt KC and Dingle Foot MP), and a solicitor (RG McKay). The police case rested mainly on the allegation that disturbances had occured at a similar meeting 14 months earlier held by Mrs Duncan at a nearby training centre and that the officer on this occasion was duty bound to prevent a repetition of such an event.

Though the appeal was lost, as was an appeal to the Divisional Court in 1936, as Kidd later observed, the decision created the precedent 'that the police have the power to ban any political meeting in streets or public places at will: no matter that such meetings are held in blind alleys where they

cannot interfere with traffic; no matter that they are peacefully conducted...'
Pritt, who had become MP for North Hammersmith in 1935, raised the matter
in a speech in the House of Commons on 10 July 1936, but to no avail.[25]

However, the public order implications of the case, though serious, paled
into insignificance compared with Government responses to the development
of fascism in Britain.

Fascism and public order

The rise of fascism and anti-semitism were major concerns for NCCL, which
quickly became, and remained for many years essentially an anti-fascist organisation. This opposition was based both on a philosophical opposition
to any organisation advocating the withholding of the freedoms of others
and deep concerns arising from the tactics adopted by fascist and far-right
groups, as well as from the response of Government to controlling public
order.

The leader of Britain's fascists was Sir Oswald Mosley, who had the distinction of having been a Conservative MP, and a member of the 1929 Labour
Government. He left to form his own New Party, which soon became the
British Union of Fascists (BUF) whose members were characterised by their
Blackshirt 'uniforms'. Violence broke out at Mosley's first major rally, held
in Manchester's Free Trade Hall in March 1933, and this set the pattern for
future events. A major BUF meeting at Olympia on 7 June 1934 was disrupted
by Communist Party and other hecklers, who were then attacked by Mosley's
Blackshirts. Whilst the NCCL publicly condemned such tactics, at least one
person wrote to Kidd to complain that the Council was biased, was only
interested in fascist violence and failed to support the 11 fascists who repor-
tedly ended up in hospital. A Mr Donald O'Connor of Dulwich pointed out
that 'organised breaking-up of meetings' was also 'an infringement of civil
liberties'. In replying, Kidd asked for evidence but doubted that there was
any. O'Connor, answering on 19 June, was blunt:

> I charge you with having, as Secretary of a pretentiously-styled Council,
> disdained even the appearance of impartiality... If an organised band of
> young hooligans arm themselves and attend a meeting with the purpose
> of breaking it up it would appear that they are at least as culpable as the
> organised young hooligans who threw them out.

The Olympia meeting was investigated by an NCCL Commission on 10/11
July 1934, chaired (again) by Aylmer Digby KC. This clearly assigned blame

to Mosley's followers and was sharply critical of the police for not intervening to protect anti-fascists.[26] However, the accusation of bias did not go away and the dilemma started by Donald O'Connor has exercised the minds of many NCCL members ever since.

The riots and brawls associated with fascism and anti-fascism, largely concentrated in the East End of London, eventually led to the Public Order Act of 1936. The main provision of this Act was to make it an offence to wear political uniforms in public but it also, amongst other things, gave the police the power to ban demonstrations themselves, without having to consult magistrates, as long as they feared public disorder. In addition to this obvious threat to freedom of assembly, one section of the Act also increased the maximum fine for the use of threatening or insulting words and behaviour from £2 to £50.

Such increased power was first used following incidents at Stepney Green on 14 July 1937, when the police made a baton charge on a crowd attending a fascist meeting in the heart of a Jewish residential area. A large proportion of the crowd was actually Jewish, watching mainly out of curiosity. At the same meeting the police attempted to prevent heckling and a passer-by who whistled at the crowd was arrested and charged with insulting behaviour. Another resident, sent by his wife to find their young daughter, blew his nose 'in an offensive manner' near the crowd and was also arrested under the Public Order Act. Both cases were later dismissed by magistrates.[27] Such misuse of Acts intended for other purposes is another recurring theme of NCCL's case histories.

Official bias: public halls and the police

The NCCL and other anti-establishment groups often had to contend with blatant bias by public bodies, particularly in the letting of halls for meetings. The Royal Albert Hall was typically obstructive. Its controlling corporation, despite operating rent-free and with a sizeable public subsidy, had discretionary powers over lettings. Bookings were allowed for the Conservative Party, the Labour Party and the BUF, but applications by anti-fascist groups such as the Co-ordinating Committee Against Fascism, organised by John Strachey, a Communist, were refused in September 1934 and March 1935.

The CCAF received the support of NCCL, although Kidd always emphasised that NCCL had no other connection with it, for it was widely regarded as a Commmunist front organisation. Similarly, in April 1936 the Albert Hall Committee refused a meeting of the British Section of the Women's World

Committee Against War and Fascism. No grounds were given and it was even admitted that the dates requested for the meeting were available. In the same month Harry Pollitt of the Communist Party of Great Britain wrote to Kidd to report that the Hall had turned down a request from the CPGB to hold a meeting on 21 May, a date known to be free. Requests from Kidd himself in March 1937 to hold 'a great freedom rally on civil liberties' were turned down a month later, after the Hall Secretary had asked for a list of speakers to put before the Council at its next meeting. In March 1937 the Albert Hall also refused to let Sir Stafford Cripps hold a 'United Front' meeting.[28]

But it was not just in London that bias of this kind occured. For example, in September 1936 Farnborough Urban District Council refused to let their Town Hall to the local Labour Party for a meeting entitled 'The truth about Spain' on the grounds that it might cause a 'breach of the peace'. The meeting was moved to the nearby Cove Institute instead.[29]

The conduct of the police also displayed a high level of political bias. The fourth issue of NCCL's early *News Sheet* included a report on the significant increase in the number of people arrested as suspected persons (those suspected of 'frequenting or loitering in a public place with intent to commit a felony' – the so-called 'sus' law, originally aimed at vagrants, and not repealed until 1981) and the number subsequently released without charge.[30] These rose from 2,398 in 1930 to 4,834 in 1934, with over a quarter having their charges either withdrawn or dismissed.

But complaints against police behaviour went further than this and in October 1935 NCCL announced an inquiry into police conduct. A surviving paper detailed the types of irregularities considered. These included partiality, such as forbidding the sale of the *Daily Worker* in the street, lenient treatment of fascists, banning and breaking up of processions, obstruction charges, intimidation, alleged assault, treatment of witnesses, use of *agents provocateurs* and wrongful arrests.[31]

The police provided more spectacular evidence during an anti-fascist meeting on 22 March 1936 in Thurloe Square, London. The meeting was held at the same time as a Blackshirt rally was taking place in the nearby Albert Hall and speakers pointed out that the Hall management had repeatedly refused to let to anti-fascists. By pure chance, Captain the Hon. Arthur Hope, Unionist MP for Aston in Birmingham, was visiting his mother in Thurloe Square at the very same time, and appears to have complained to the police about the threat made by the crowd to his car. For reasons which still remain a mystery, the police, some on horseback, then advanced on and baton-charged the crowd without warning. The Home Secretary, Sir John Simon, refused to allow a public inquiry, although during the debate in the House of Commons he referred more than once to 'my honourable friend's motor car'.

However, the NCCL organised its own inquiry, having obtained statements from 113 witnesses. Its Commission included two professors (one of whom, Norman Bentwich, acted as Chair), a barrister, a Quaker businessman, Eleanor Rathbone MP, and the writer JB Priestley. The inquiry was held at Friends' Meeting House on Friday 10 July and Tuesday 14 July 1936, and the surviving minutes of proceedings run to two volumes of shorthand notes. Evidence was taken from 31 witnesses, including nine official NCCL observers, and such figures as John Strachey and the Reverend Stanley Evans. The Commission found that the baton charge was unprovoked and unnecessary and that charges of police brutality were substantiated. Despite a foreword by Harold Laski, the Report made little impact when published.[32]

The British public was doubtless, and understandably, more concerned with the momentous happenings in the Spanish Civil War and the abdication of Edward VIII, while the Home Secretary was still refusing to allow an official inquiry into Northern Ireland. If the (extremely biased) advice he received from the Commissioner of Police, commenting on the NCCL and its Thurloe Square report in September 1936 is anything to go by, the reasons for this refusal are clear:

> This is a self-constituted body with no authority or statutory powers, whose principal activity is to criticise and attack the police on every opportunity they can find or make, and which has arrogated to itself the right to set up Commissions to inquire into the actions of constituted authorities in the exercise of their responsibility. If they are accorded an inquiry it will give them some status and encourage their troublesome activities, which have, I think it is true to say, no public backing whatever.[33]

Biased officials: the Harworth Colliery dispute, 1937

Probably the most serious example of police and judicial bias during this period was the Harworth Colliery affair of 1937, which, coincidentally, provided ample evidence of 'public backing' for NCCL.

Harworth Colliery, Bawtry, was owned by Barber & Walkers Limited, who also owned six other mines in Nottinghamshire and Yorkshire. In late 1935 a pay claim by the Nottinghamshire Miners' Association was opposed by the employers and the rival Spencer Union (the Nottinghamshire and District

Miners' Industrial Union, set up by the Labour MP and trade union official, George Spencer, during the General Strike of 1926 and subsequently developed as a company union by the employers). In November 1936 a ballot indicated that of the miners at Harworth 1,175 wished to belong to the NMA, and only 145 to the Spencer Union. However, the management imposed membership of the latter as a condition of employment and men were asked to sign a form authorising deductions for this purpose from their wages. Many who refused were locked out and replaced. Matters were brought to a head by an official strike which started in September 1936 over the sacking of two men for a refreshment break.

Kidd paid his first visit to the NMA's offices at Old Basford, Nottingham, in late January 1937, following the receipt of reports about the conduct of police towards the striking miners. Strikers and their families had been ordered to stay indoors, had been harassed and fined for petty offences. Kidd made his own report to the NCCL in March 1937, and this was published after careful checking by legal advisers William A Jowitt and Sir Stafford Cripps KC MP, for possible libel.

Public attention was further increased by the visit of actors Sybil Thorndike, Lewis Casson, and others, belonging to the theatre company of Llewellyn Rees, who visited Harworth in early April during a break from performing in Nottingham. Rees wrote to Kidd on 8 April saying, 'I thought it might interest you and the Council to know that a man came up to me only about five minutes after our arrival and said "If you had come down here before Mr Roland [sic] Kidd came from London you would have had the police taking names and addresses by now".'

On 23/24 April, many strikers, including the leaders, were arrested during what were depicted by the police as major disturbances in the village.

Kidd visited the area again, this time with Geoffrey Bing, on the weekend of Saturday 1 May and, amongst others, met a Mr W Pennington, who happened to own the Market Hall in Harworth where the most serious incidents were said to have taken place. On 3 May Pennington, describing himself as an ex-Army officer who voted Conservative and was on good terms with the colliery owners, sent Kidd his own detailed report on the events. He had discovered from reliable witnesses that:

> The disturbances and raid were caused by the Police themselves, the whole affair was planned, so that it would cause a riot and so that the blame for such riot would be fastened on to the Miners but, unfortunately for the Police, there were too many independent persons who witnessed

them deliberately smash the windows and door of the Market Hall with their batons...[34]

The trials of 33 miners took place at Worksop and, of these, 17 were sent to the assizes at Nottingham in May and June. Kidd secured the services of Cripps to defend the miners at Worksop Police Court though this did not prevent the imposition of severe sentences, with the strike leader, Michael Kane, president of the Harworth branch of the NMA, receiving two years, and 12 others receiving between four and 15 months. This aroused considerable public indignation and NCCL organised a petition for remission of the sentences. Launched on 9 July and produced with the co-operation of the Trades Union Congress, London Trades Council and the Mineworkers' Federation of Great Britain, it contained 250,880 signatures when it was presented to the Home Secretary on 8 September. Unfortunately, the result was merely a slight remission in sentences.

In presenting the case for the Harworth men, the NCCL laid emphasis on the obvious bias of magistrates in favour of their peers – in this case mine-owners. Such behaviour was again apparent in 'The strange case of Major Vernon' later in 1937.

The Vernon case

According to the 1936 edition of *The Civil Service Compendium,* civil servants then, as now, were 'free to belong to any political party – Conservative, Liberal, Labour, or Communist'. In 1937 NCCL and the National Union of Journalists launched a campaign against the misuse of the Official Secrets Act.

Major Wilfred Foulston Vernon, aged 54, a man with a distinguished war record, who had been a technical officer at the Royal Aircraft Establishment in Farnborough since 1925, unwittingly focused attention on the problem this caused. Vernon had been an active socialist since 1921 and was a member of the League of Nations Union. In the summer of 1937 four men broke into his Farnborough home and were apprehended while he was away on holiday. In their defence, they claimed to be fascists acting for political reasons in order to reveal a subversive in government service. In fact, they had stolen left-wing books, but also private documents, cutlery, a watch, money, a telescope and a travelling rug. In an extraordinary turn-about, reports of the resulting committal hearings and court case suggest that, rather than the four men being on trial for common theft, it was Vernon who was on trial for his political opinions.[35]

The laws of evidence were flagrantly ignored by the Chair of the Court. One defendant, J Ford, claimed that in 1934 he had conspired with Vernon to spread Communist propaganda amongst the troops at Aldershot. Vernon denied this. Despite being found guilty of 'larceny in a dwellinghouse', the four received very light sentences, being bound over for 12 months. Vernon, however, was immediately suspended from his post for acting 'prejudiciously to the Service'. Amongst the papers stolen from Vernon's house were some drawings and sketches relating to his RAE work. These mysteriously came into the possession of the Air Ministry, which prosecuted Vernon under the Official Secrets Act of 1920. Vernon, defended by DN Pritt, pleaded guilty when the case was heard at Farnham Magistrates' Court on 23 October 1937, was fined £50, and promptly dismissed from the Civil Service on 13 November. He spent most of the war years as an instructor for the Home Guard, and was eventually elected to Parliament for the Labour Party in 1945. The NCCL's pamphlet about the affair was entitled, most appropriately, *The Strange Case of Major Vernon*.

The Vernon case was also an outstanding example of the problems of what were then called 'black-coated workers'. Kidd produced an article on 'Civil rights and the Civil Servant' for *New Outlook* in February 1938. A conference on the same topic was called by NCCL for 10 December 1938 in London but had to be postponed owing to a breakdown in Kidd's health, which had deteriorated since he had been knocked down by a car in November 1937. This not only resulted in a broken leg but revealed an irregular heart condition, the discovery of which led his doctor to advise Kidd to slow down.[36] The conference was eventually held on 18 February 1939. It was concerned particularly with the tendency of banks, insurance companies and government departments to act against free and independent trade unions and attempts to debar teachers from all forms of political activity.

Consolidation

The 'surge' of Mosley and the BUF more or less ended at the March 1937 London County Council elections when none of the 40 fascist candidates were elected. Mosley was forced to cut his salaried staff from 143 to 30, and two of those axed, John Beckett and William Joyce, set up a rival group. Whilst remaining ever vigilant against the fascist threat, NCCL was now able to expand its activities into other areas of general concern.

By the late 1930s the organisation had become firmly established. The distinguished liberal writer, Henry Nevinson, had replaced Forster as President and there was still an array of 59 'celebrity' Vice-Presidents. The Executive Committee, elected at the Annual General Meeting, in February 1939, consisted of four MPs (Sir Richard Acland, Barnstaple, Arthur Creech Jones, Shipley, DN Pritt, North Hammersmith, and Wilfrid Roberts, Northern Cumberland); six barristers; four solicitors; an author (Mrs Haden Guest); and two journalists (EE Hunter and Kingsley Martin). There were also six Sub-Committees:

— **General Purposes:** which met weekly to deal with administrative and financial matters

— **Legal:** which dealt with cases and provided legal advice

— **British Overseas:** concerned with Indian, Colonial and Dominion civil liberties

— **Foreign:** concerned with international civil rights and, in particular, the right of asylum

— **Publications:** responsible for producing journals, pamphlets and leaflets

— **Members' Activities:** which organised conferences, meetings and social activities.

The Executive Committee met monthly to review the work of the Sub-Committees and to direct policy. Branches had been established in Bristol, Cambridge, Liverpool, Manchester and Swansea and the national organisation also had 424 affiliated societies. Communication with the branches and membership was greatly improved by the Council's establishment of its own permanent newsletters or journals, the first of which was the ostensibly independent *Free Speech & Assembly Bulletin,* begun in early 1934, but published from the NCCL's offices. In its final issue (number 27) in July 1937 it was announced that the *Bulletin* would cease and be incorporated into a new official publication issued by the NCCL from September 1937 and called *Civil Liberty.* This also incorporated NCCL's *News Sheet,* which first appeared in August 1935 and survived for five issues until January 1937. *Civil Liberty* subsequently appeared at varying intervals (sometimes quarterly, bi-monthly, or even annually – effectively as an annual report), becoming *Rights* in September 1976, *Civil Liberty* again in February 1985, and *Civil Liberty Agenda* in 1991.

NCCL's nomadic existence continued throughout the 1930s and beyond, as leases expired and staff numbers varied. In April 1935 new offices, comprising two small rooms at the top of four flights of stairs, were found at 99a Charing Cross Road, WC2. Sylvia Crowther-Smith recalled that the area was noted for its prostitutes, with a large madam regularly based at the foot of the stone stairs every night.[37] Office conditions remained cramped and the Executive Committee had to hold its regular Thursday meetings in rooms elsewhere. The next move was in January 1937 to Morley House, 320 Regent Street, W1. This was on the sixth floor of a block near the British Broadcasting Corporation. Here there was a suite of three rooms with considerably more space. Indeed, in January 1937, *News Sheet* number 5 included an appeal for equipment to fill the new offices – 12 folding office chairs, an electric kettle, three cupboards for stationery, metal filing cabinets, rugs for the floors and three small tables were urgently required. In January 1940 still larger offices were taken at 37 Great James Street, Bedford Row, WC1. These were badly damaged by a landmine in 1941 and in November of that year there was another move to 11a Kings Road, Sloane Square, SW7. NCCL remained in these much larger offices until November 1949.

In the late 1930s NCCL still did not have sufficient office staff to cope with demands. Indeed, on 21 November 1938 Kidd sent a memorandum to members on the need both for office reorganisation and more staff. He explained the problems of operating with just four full-time staff (Secretary, Assistant Secretary and two typists) describing the daily residue of uncompleted work as 'a nightmare problem'. Whilst the recent formation of the Sub-Committees, mentioned above, had helped, they had also created more office work. He called for the appointment of two extra members of staff – one administrator and one typist. He also called for a greater effort in the area of fund-raising and the establishment of a large membership base. Finally, he drew attention to the condition of his health: 'I am under medical orders not to resume the former condition of overwork. My present breakdown would make it a very serious matter if my Assistant Secretary were also to get ill through overwork.'[38]

Kidd's appeals appear to have been highly persuasive for, by the end of 1939, NCCL had a staff of nine which, by 1941, had increased to 15. By late 1940 NCCL also had about 3,000 individual members plus 700 affiliated organisations, generating an annual income of £3,592. In practice, events had conspired to generate yet more work following the emergency wartime situation which prevailed after the summer of 1939.

3 Civil liberties in wartime

In August 1939 the Emergency Powers Act was passed, enabling the government to introduce a series of 'Defence Regulations'. The most significant of these for civil liberties was Defence Regulation 18B which effectively suspended *habeas corpus*.

In general, people of overseas origin were particularly vulnerable at this time but there were 73,000 nationals of enemy countries in Britain at the outbreak of the war who were initially categorised according to their degree of 'trustworthiness'. In 1940, however, following a campaign in the *Daily Mail* and elsewhere against 'fifth columnists', the Home Office decided to intern them all. Although NCCL could do little to prevent this, it did at least investigate and draw attention to conditions in the camps. It had considerably greater success in its attempts to protect the freedom of the press.

The press and BBC

The behaviour of the BBC towards its employees and artists has been a matter of debate ever since the Corporation was established. The opportunity for over-zealous behaviour was increased at the outset of the war when the Minister for Information, Duff Cooper, reduced the number of BBC governors from five to two.

The question of anti-left bias by the employers had been brought to the fore by the People's Convention of 12 January 1941, organised by the Communist Party. A number of artists, particularly musicians, who performed for the BBC, signed the People's Convention Manifesto. Artists such as Sir Hugh Roberton (of the Glasgow Orpheus Choir) were banned from the airwaves and the BBC subsequently put pressure on all those who had signed either to disown the Convention or else see their contracts terminated. This caused outrage and a number of famous artists, including the composer Ralph Vaughan Williams, agreed to an NCCL-organised letter of protest to the press. Several, including Forster, Vaughan Williams, and the actor Michael Redgrave, also refused to take part in BBC broadcasts at the time.

George Bernard Shaw, who had recently joined the NCCL (and had been present in Trafalgar Square during the 'Bloody Sunday' episode of 1887) sent one of his typically forthright postcards offering advice to Kidd on 6 March 1941:

> The whole managing staff of the BBC should be sacked instantly. Here we are in [the] thick of a war which we claim to be fighting as the

champions of western democracy. Daily we throw in the teeth of Germany and Italy the reproach that they have abolished the rights of public meeting and free speech. And this is the moment selected by the BBC to give the world an exhibition of British Nazi-ism gone mad. Just on top of the suppression of a newspaper too! Europe will hear all about it from Herr Goebbels and W Joyce. We liquidate our looters, whose mischief is comparatively negligible. When shall we learn to liquidate our fools?

NCCL organised a protest meeting on 17 March 1941 which was addressed by Forster, Beatrix Lehmann, Llewellyn Rees, Michael Redgrave, the Archdeacon of Westminster, Phil Cardew (a band leader) and Hardie Ratcliffe (of the Musicians' Union). On 20 March the Prime Minister, Winston Churchill, announced in the House of Commons that the BBC had lifted its ban on artists who attended the People's Convention. The Minister of Information, Duff Cooper, also immediately reconstituted the BBC's Board of Governors, including two new non-Conservative members, Dr J J Mallon and Lady Violet Bonham-Carter. Nevinson wrote to Kidd on 31 March saying, 'We – I mean you – are to be congratulated on our triumph over the BBC.'[39]

Political suspicions

Shaw's mention of 'the suppression of a newspaper' was a reference to the Government's suppression of the *Daily Worker* under Defence Regulation 2D (which covered the fomenting of opposition to the war) in early 1941. In March the NCCL's Executive Committee issued a statement attacking the Government over this. The ban was lifted in the summer of 1942 but NCCL's stance immediately led to renewed charges of Communist allegiance.[40]

Almost from the start, in fact, NCCL had been dogged by such accusations, and of being a front for the Communist Party. Indeed, for some, association with the Council was enough to confirm guilt. As early as the Labour Party Annual Conference at Southport on 1 October 1934 (when expulsion of undesirable far-left elements was starting to become popular) Aneurin Bevan had asked 'Are you going to expel Mr Lansbury, Major Attlee, and Mr Wall (Secretary of the London Trades and Labour Council) for associating with Communists on the Council for Civil Liberties?'

On 16 November 1934, Vyvyan Adams, the only Conservative MP who was a Vice-President of NCCL, resigned. In a letter to Forster, he observed, 'You will appreciate that it is difficult for me so to continue, as I am the only Conservative who officially belongs to the Council. Had you succeeded in getting other Conservative Vice-Presidents this difficulty would probably not have arisen.'[41]

Part of the problem was that certain leading members of NCCL were indeed either Communists (such as Claud Cockburn) or close associates. One individual who attracted considerable long-term attention in this regard was DN Pritt, who apart from being a member of the NCCL's Executive Committee between 1934 and 1960, also served as a legal adviser to the CPGB and was later a member of the Labour Party's National Executive Committee between 1937 and 1940, before he was expelled from the Labour Party for denouncing the 'imperialist war'. Forster was always deeply conscious of charges of bias. When, in January 1935, the NCCL drew up a declaration of principles, he managed, against much opposition, to impose an impartial stance. The draft declaration had referred to the threat to civil liberty 'from whatever quarter', but Forster changed this to 'the threat from left or right'.

If members of the public were sceptical about the NCCL's true allegiance, then the police and security services had no doubts. Surveillance of leading members had taken place from the beginning. Metropolitan Police files from the 1930s, now held in the Public Record Office, show the extent to which NCCL was regarded as a Communist front organisation, and Kidd a major trouble maker. One file, entitled 'Activities of Ronald Kidd, Secretary of NCCL 1930-36', described him as 'not a man on whom any reliance can be placed'. This file was opened in November 1930, when Kidd made a voluntary statement after witnessing a motor accident in Chandos Street in London. In January 1933 Special Branch reported that he was a member of the West Central London Branch of the Friends of the Soviet Union. Thereafter, he appears to have been labelled a communist by the police, whose views were confirmed by his occasional appearances on platforms with the likes of Willie Gallacher, Harry Pollitt and John Gollan of the CPGB.

Members of NCCL were routinely placed under surveillance, correspondence was intercepted and copied, and meetings were 'overheard'. Reports summarising Kidd's movements were initially compiled by Special Branch every three months but from November 1935 Kidd's file was updated weekly, at the request of the Commissioner of Police. The Metropolitan Police files even include copies of letters taken from the NCCL offices *before* they had been posted. These, plus records of internal meetings, suggest that the NCCL had been infiltrated by the police at a high level.[42]

Surveillance of NCCL's senior staff appears to have been routinely undertaken ever since. In May 1990, Harriet Harman (Legal Officer) and Patricia Hewitt (General Secretary), appealed to the European Commission of Human

Rights over the fact that they had been under surveillance by the intelligence service, MI5, whilst working for NCCL in the 1970s. They won their case against the British Government but still did not gain sight of their files.[43] However, their original complaint prompted the Government to pass the Security Service Act 1989, placing MI5 on a statutory basis for the first time.

Meanwhile, Ronald Kidd regularly had to fend off charges that the NCCL was a front for the Communist Party. Members being asked to renew their subscriptions sought reassurance on this point. The National Council of Labour, a fairly reactionary body in any case under Sir Walter Citrine, was deeply suspicious of the NCCL, and took particular exception to the proposed conference of 24 August 1940 on 'Civil Liberty and the Defeat of Fascism', which followed a successful emergency conference on 21 July of over 1500 delegates, principally from trade unions, representing nearly two million people. An NCL circular letter of 9 August challenged NCCL's apparent claim to represent the labour movement and queried its political allegiance. In reply, Nevinson and Kidd pointed out that NCCL was 'a non-party and non-political organisation whose objects are publicly stated and whose members represent many different schools of thought. Our list of Vice-Presidents is sufficient evidence of this statement.'[44]

One of the dangers of having so many high-profile Vice-Presidents was demonstrated in mid-March 1941 when Kidd was surprised to discover a report in the press that the Liberal MP, Harcourt Johnson, had 'resigned as a Vice-President on 14 March' on the grounds that DN Pritt, also a Vice-President and EC member, was allegedly a Communist. Kidd issued a press release noting that Johnson's position as a Vice-President had lapsed some years earlier, so he could hardly resign. Nevertheless, he was not the last high-profile officer to renounce the organisation in this way.

Pritt inevitably attracted the most criticism. On 25 May 1941 LH Green of Richmond, Surrey, complained about NCCL's links with and support for, the People's Convention and about Pritt's communism. In reply, Kidd expressed himself 'amazed', and denied any link with the Convention. Answering on 7 June, Green referred to Pritt as 'an active and notorious Communist'. On 26 June Kidd again defended Pritt, noting that he was a member of the Labour Party and saying also, 'It would appear to be rather anomalous for a body which stands predominantly for freedom of opinion to chuck out an eminent KC who has been of enormous help on our legal cases, merely because his political views may have become increasingly unpopular – the more so as we are a non-political, non-party organisation... Personally I myself am not and never have been a Communist.'

Yet another member, Arnold Palmer, also wrote to Kidd a week later on 3 July 1941 to complain about Pritt. Mr Palmer was under the impression that Pritt had only recently become a Vice-President and EC member. He wondered if his name on NCCL's notepaper might be balanced by adding that of Rudolf Hess – 'that would show that the Council's tolerance, however mistaken, was at least complete.'

Attacks from rank and file members and ex-Vice-Presidents could be dealt with. But a particular blow came with the arrival of the corrected proofs of a new pamphlet called *The Freedom of the Press* by Harold Laski on 16 May 1941, accompanied by his letter of resignation. Laski pleaded pressure of work but also an unwillingness to serve on a body 'which contains Communist members'. In reply (26 May) Kidd reasserted that the Council was 'a non-party organisation... open to all shades of religious and political opinion (including Communists). We have no knowledge of the political convictions of our members and we are under the impression that we have no Communist members on our Executive Committee.' Laski's resignation may have seemed difficult to understand given the way he was himself publicly perceived as a Communist fellow-traveller at the time.

More was to come. At the Labour Party Conference (opened 2 June 1941) when AM Wall (Secretary of the London Society of Compositors and for 12 years Secretary of the London Trades Council, who had resigned as a Vice-President of the NCCL in 1939) claimed that NCCL was almost entirely under Communist Party control. A letter denying this under the signatures of Nevinson, Forster and others was sent to the press on 18 June 1941 and appeared in *The New Statesman, Time & Tide*, and elsewhere. It stated: 'Mr Wall has been misinformed about this matter, and we take the opportunity of categorically denying the statement which he made. This organisation is not and never has been under Communist control and, as long as we are associated with it, it will not be under that or any other political domination.' The editor of *Time & Tide* (Lady Rhondda) added a note saying that, in her opinion, Wall's perception was more believable than that of innocents like Nevinson and Forster.

In a scribbled and undated note sent to Kidd, probably in June 1941, Pritt offered to resign, adding:

> To trot out the communist bogey is the.oldest and rottenest trick of reaction. Ever since political controversy began the Right have always labelled every movement or activity tending to serve the cause of progress with whatever left-wing label is for the time being unpopular

– radical, liberal, labour, socialist, communist. It saves trouble, it saves thought, it saves making out a case, or answering the progressive case on the merits; and often enough you can even get away with condemning criticism as 'communist' at the same time as you tacitly admit the soundness of the communist criticism by trying to remedy the grievance criticised. It also has the advantage that you can label anyone communist who is doing anything active when you want to keep a dunghill covered.

In a further development, an editorial in *Time & Tide* on 28 June asked Forster, amongst other things, to deny that at an EC meeting of NCCL in February two leading members had protested against alleged Communist influence. Forster did not answer this charge but, in a letter to him on 27 June, Kidd explained that the February EC meeting had discussed a draft press statement regarding the suppression of the *Daily Worker*. The version finally agreed had been drawn up by Harold Laski and Kingsley Martin and Kidd, in fact, suspected that the latter was the real author of the critical remarks in *Time & Tide*. In the 5 July issue of *Time & Tide* Rebecca West joined the fray, describing the NCCL as 'dewy, cloistered, nun-like', and explaining that she had resigned as a Vice-President in 1940 in protest against the campaign – run, she suggested, purely for Communist ends – over conditions in French internment camps.

On 23 July, the writer Owen Rattenbury, a NCCL member wrote to Kidd about the extent of Communist Party influence. Indignant, Kidd replied at length on 28 July, pointing out that the political views of NCCL staff were none of his (Kidd's) business, and that 'So long as I am General Secretary there will always continue to be only one test for employees in this office – not a doctrinal one, but simply, do they take a genuine interest in our work, and do they do their jobs conscientiously?' Kidd claimed he could not say which, if any, of his staff was a Communist but, most certainly, he was not: 'I am not and have never been a Communist.'[45]

The end of an era

Unfortunately, Kidd's days as General Secretary were numbered. Although his most important book, *British Liberty in Danger*, was well received on its publication in August 1940, its author was in very poor health and getting worse. In addition, despite a remarkable surge in the first two years of the war, NCCL's finances had again become critical and though staff numbers had risen to 15, cuts were now thought necessary. The seriousness of the situation was emphasised when *Civil Liberty* appeared in September 1941 as a two-paged cyclo-styled sheet with an appeal for funds. This shocked members, as perhaps was intended.

In August 1941 Sylvia Crowther-Smith resigned as Assistant Secretary, although she remained a member of the Executive Committee until the mid-1950s. She later recalled that her resignation was mainly because of her ailing mother (who was dying from cancer) and Kidd's continuing poor health.[46] In fact, Kidd had been unable to perform his duties for some months following a recurrence of his heart condition in January 1941, and Nancy Bell (who joined NCCL as National Organiser in October 1940) had deputised for him in his absence.

Kidd was 'promoted' to the new post of Director in November 1941, with Elizabeth Acland Allen taking over as General Secretary. She had joined the staff earlier in 1941 as Appeals Officer after some years as Joint Secretary of the International Peace Campaign in Geneva. She had also been a member of the Executive Committee of the Women's Liberal Federation and one of the organisers of the Brussels Peace Conference in 1936. WH Thompson had suggested that Kidd might become President, replacing Nevinson, who had died on 9 November, but Kidd, always a modest man, thought he lacked the necessary stature. Forster resumed the Presidency in 1942 (for one year only). Thereafter the post lapsed until 1966.

At a memorial meeting for Nevinson, held at Caxton Hall on 11 December, Kidd appeared on the platform as Director, and Elizabeth Allen as General Secretary. And although his health continued to deteriorate, Kidd did manage to complete a pamphlet on the freedom of the press, which was published in March 1942.[47] He died on 12 May 1942 at the age of 53 and was cremated at Golders Green Crematorium three days later, where the tributes were led by Forster.[48] In an appreciation of Kidd in *Civil Liberty*, Kingsley Martin described him as 'the last Edwardian Bohemian' who had a spontaneous resentment for authority. Martin also gave an 'Empire Broadcast' on the BBC in appreciation of Kidd on 15 May 1942. Two years later, in the summer of 1944, a memorial plaque carved in mahogany by the eminent artist Jesse Collins was unveiled in NCCL's offices at 11a Kings Road. The words were written by Forster:

RONALD KIDD 1889-1942

He founded our Council in 1934 and was its first Secretary. It is his memorial. Passionate in his hatred of injustice, wise in judgement, fearless in action, he championed the liberties of the people in the fight that is never done.

The release of Mosley

Elizabeth Allen's initial enthusiasm was directed at anti-fascist work. In particular, she warned against fascism's revival, most notably in the pamphlet *It Shall Not Happen Here: Anti-Semitism, Fascists and Civil Liberty,* which was produced in 1943 and had sold 25,000 copies by the end of the war. In March that year an associated conference on this subject attracted 443 delegates.

Oswald Mosley and 200 of his followers had been detained in May 1940 under Defence Regulation 18B, which at its introduction had been denounced by NCCL, the Communist Party and others. Now, the Government's decision to release Mosley led both the Communist Party and NCCL to call for him to be re-interned, arguing that he was the country's leading fascist and that his release was ordered on the grounds of class privilege rather than poor health, as claimed. An emergency meeting of the Executive Committee on 19 November 1943 adopted a resolution deploring the decision to release Moseley and his wife. It stated that 'this step must create the most profound disquiet in the minds of all those who are fighting or working against fascism and who know that its survival either in this country or abroad threatens all our civil liberties.'

The NCCL received many letters of support but even more of protest from people who pointed out that it was not the business of NCCL to advocate the continued imprisonment of people without trial.[49] In a debate on Mosley in the House of Commons on 1 December 1943 the Home Secretary, Herbert Morrison, asserted that the release was purely for medical reasons. Describing NCCL disparagingly as 'an amazing organisation', he noted that it, along with the Communist Party, had 'switched right round' from its earlier position.[50] In the ensuing vote, 62 MPs (including DN Pritt) voted against the government, most of them either Labour Party, Independent Labour Party or Communist Party members – all of whom had previously opposed the principle of detention without trial.

On 21 December the Hon. Harold Nicolson MP wrote to Allen, saying 'It seems illogical to me that a body calling itself the Council for Civil Liberties should support the theory that any citizen can be kept in prison without trial. I should imagine that every thinking person realised that *habeas corpus* was the foundation of our civil liberties and that 18B was their negation... I can no longer remain associated with a Council whose Executive takes action contrary to the purposes which (I had supposed) the Council had in mind.' Though Nicolson was not actually a member, a total of 39 individual members did resign in protest between December 1943 and June 1944.[51]

New faces, old problems

Having repeatedly been accused of supporting Communists, NCCL now upset supporters of the pacifist cause by declining to support individuals who had broken the law. The Peace Pledge Union, for example, resigned its membership in June 1944, a decision which was chiefly connected with the case of George Elphick, a conscientious objector, who had been summonsed to Lewes Police Court nine times for refusing to comply with fire watching regulations. On 21 July 1944 Elizabeth Allen wrote to the Secretary of the Central Board for Conscientious Objectors explaining that the NCCL could not campaign 'on behalf of someone who has admittedly broken the law'.[52] This led to an article in *The Tribunal: Independent War-Resisters' Forum* in August 1944 entitled 'What's wrong with the NCCL?' which commented, with respect to the Elphick case: 'We are driven to believe that something exceedingly rotten has eaten into the Council, destroying its capacity to fulfil its functions.' There immediately followed an article by CEM Joad (another NCCL Vice-President) in the Central Board for Conscientious Objectors' *Bulletin* of September 1944, entitled (harking back to Major Vernon) 'The strange case of the Council for Civil Liberties'.[53]

The NCCL's Executive Committee was sharply divided on this matter. Kingsley Martin wrote to Allen on 23 September saying 'No issue of civil liberty would ever have been won if its champions had not been willing to support people who had infringed the law, and nobody knows this better than the NCCL.' In a letter to Allen on 11 August RSW Pollard put forward a motion resolving that a breach of the law 'is no bar to a case being taken up by the NCCL' and a statement to this effect was adopted by the EC on 26 September 1944.[54]

The Council's mysterious response to a case resulting from the Tyneside apprentices' strike in 1944 is also interesting – given the mutual hatred between the Communist Party and Trotskyists. In late 1944 NCCL was accused by the Revolutionary Communist Party of failing to help Trotskyists charged under the Trade Disputes Act 1927 in connection with the Tyneside apprentices strike and the arrest of Heaton Lee, Ann Keen and Roy Tearse. The EC's views were minuted thus: 'After considerable discussion it was agreed that a letter should be sent asking in what respect their democratic and legal rights were being challenged by the use of this Act.'[55] In the event, the strikers received no support from NCCL.

4 Peace, but no rest

The deaths of major figures like Kidd and Nevinson, followed by the political divisions which surfaced during the latter part of the war, did not leave NCCL in a very strong position when peace emerged in May 1945. Matters were not helped by the long ill health of Nancy Bell and her eventual resignation as national organiser in May 1946. She died in March 1947. As for WH Thompson, mentioned earlier, her importance to the organisation has often been forgotten. At the time, however, she received the same salary as the General Secretary and was sorely missed.

Democratic rights for the armed forces

The harsh manner in which the army dealt with the Cairo Forces Parliament – a spontaneous body established as a means of promoting thought and discussion amongst members of the British forces based in Egypt – succeeded in drawing attention to the negligible rights of ordinary soldiers, most of whom had been conscripted.[56]

The NCCL's concern arose largely from the decision of the Government to persist with conscription in peacetime. In December 1946 there were still over 1.4 million men in the British armed forces (compared with about 450,000 during the inter-war years). Many were stationed in countries of the British Empire – particularly India, Palestine, Egypt and Malaya. An important campaign meeting was held at the Palace Theatre, Cambridge Circus, on Sunday 10 November 1946 when the speakers included a young Lieutenant LJ Callaghan (later the Labour Prime Minister), ex-Staff Sergeant RJ Spector and DN Pritt. Questions such as the revision of the military code, improved education and welfare services, and the right of free voluntary association and discussion were debated.[57] In 1946 this interest led to the establishment of the Lewis Committee to review court martial procedures, which reported in 1949. The campaign was revived in a slightly different form during the 1960s.

Communists again:
declining support and the departure of EM Forster

Visible signs of public support for the activities of NCCL appeared to decline noticeably once the war was over. For example, one of its major initiatives was the organisation of an International Conference on Human Rights in London in June 1947. Whilst during the initial planning stages it was hoped that hundreds of delegates would appear, in the event only 69 turned up, representing just 15 countries and four British colonies. And only 147 people attended the Annual General Meeting of NCCL held in March 1948, in contrast to the many hundreds which had been the norm in earlier years of the decade.

The main issue at that particular AGM was political discrimination in the civil service against communists and others of the left. Naturally, it was not long before the question of NCCL's motives in discussing such matters came under scrutiny. The EC elected for 1947/48 was dominated by socialists (including Angela Tuckett, Pritt and Reginald Bridgeman, who were widely assumed to be Communist Party members) and trade union representatives, of whom there were 10. In sharp contrast to earlier years, there were only three barristers (including Pritt) and one solicitor (Tuckett). On 17 September 1947 William S Shepherd MP wrote to Allen stating that he was preparing a publication on 'Crypto-communist organisations' and wanted information regarding the number of non-communists or socialists in membership. Allen replied on 10 October emphasising the NCCL's non-party and non-sectarian role. On 14 October Shepherd wrote back suggesting that 'you ought to be renamed The National Council for *Some* Civil Liberties'.[58]

The issue of Communist influence also prompted EM Forster to quit the Council. He formally resigned his membership in a letter to Allen on 30 April 1948 but in a letter to the *New Statesman,* published on 15 May, he explained that he had resigned because of a resolution at the recent AGM censuring the Government for its proposed purge of Communists in key public jobs, which he regarded as a political rather than a civil liberties matter. In a further letter to the *New Statesman* on 5 June, Forster clarified his position, saying that, whereas in the earlier case of Major Vernon an individual's civil liberties had been involved, members of NCCL were now expected to offer general support to groups like the Communist Party: 'Communists themselves might very properly propose such a vote of censure, but it seemed to me inadmissible in the agenda of a non-party body, so I reluctantly resigned.'

Forster was followed by Lady Artemus-Jones on 20 May 'for reasons similar to those given by Mr EM Forster'.[59] In fact, along with George Orwell, Bertrand Russell and others, Forster went on to join a short-lived rival to NCCL called the Freedom Defence Committee.

Naturally, unsympathetic journalists made the most of such a major loss from NCCL's ranks. The editor of *The Spectator* commented on 21 May:

> I am not surprised that Mr EM Forster has resigned from the National Council for Civil Liberties. I shall only be surprised if his resignation is not followed by others. This body has been moving visibly to the Left

for some time, and it now appears that it is thoroughly pervaded by Communist influence. Mr Forster stands well to the Left in politics himself, and if he finds the present flavour of the Council of Civil Liberties is too strong for him I imagine it will be too strong for most people.[60]

The 'communist charge' has emerged fairly regularly ever since, although much less so after the 1970s. In June 1951 Professor Norman Bentwich resigned from the NCCL on the grounds that it was 'conducted in the interest of the Communist Party'. An editorial in *The Spectator* on 12 July 1957 stated that the Executive Committee of NCCL included 'three well known Communists and 10 others who are associated with organisations which have been proscribed by the Labour Party.'[61]

To make matters worse, 1948 was a year of serious financial crisis for the Council, necessitating drastic reductions in staff and office accommodation. There was an urgent appeal for funds in the July/August issue of *Civil Liberty*, which also included commercial advertisements for the first time. The September issue carried a warning from Elizabeth Allen that it might be necessary to produce a curtailed issue of *Civil Liberty* similar to that of September 1941 if sufficient funds were not forthcoming. In retrospect, it is clear that a major campaign was needed in order to restore NCCL's credibility and appeal. By chance, a suitable issue had already been discovered.

Mental health

The NCCL initiated and led the nationwide campaign for the reform of the Mental Deficiency Act of 1913. This Act allowed people to be classed as mentally deficient on dubious grounds, including becoming pregnant when unmarried – such people being described as 'moral defectives'. An almost secret system had grown up which appeared routinely to permit widespread abuse and had allowed the incarceration, often for many years, of men, women and, far too often, children who did not have mental problems.

As early as 1947 NCCL had taken up the case of 'Jane', who had been detained in a senile ward having given birth to an illegitimate child and then been refused shelter by her father.[62] The stories behind 12 similar cases were presented to an NCCL Conference on Mental Deficiency held on 10 June 1950 at which more than 200 representatives were present. This was followed in 1951 by the publication of the pamphlet, *50,000 Outside the Law*, which claimed that five out of six cases did not involve mental deficiency at all. Publication of this pamphlet prompted widespread press coverage of the topic for the first time and the *Glasgow Herald* described NCCL as 'the un-official keepers of the public conscience'.

A second conference was held on mental deficiency laws in the Summer of 1951. This resolved 'that the existing law and system of administration relating to mental deficiency does not conform to the best interest of the community and is at variance with the rights of citizens to personal freedom...'. The Conference called for a public inquiry, for which NCCL received support in *The Lancet* and *Medical World.*

Meanwhile more cases came to light, including that of a man of 39, of above average intelligence and no criminal record, who had been held for 24 years on the basis of a story told by relatives when he was 15. It was also apparent that many inmates in mental homes were in fact being used as cheap labour in order to subsidise the running of such homes. The *Annual Report* for 1954/55 noted the case of 'Ivy', a girl of 15 who had been backward at school but not 'sub-normal'. She had appeared before a juvenile court for a minor offence and was then detained under the Mental Deficiency Act. She ended up ironing sheets for three shillings a week and was held for five years, having had her release obstructed by the Board of Control. NCCL eventually obtained a writ of *habeas corpus* in the High Court and the girl quickly obtained a factory job.

The case of Kathleen Rutty attracted even more publicity. She had been illegally detained for seven years. Having lived in institutions from the age of three months to 17 years, she was later placed in a mental institution under a 'place of safety' order having been 'found neglected'. This order had not been examined by a magistrate and was therefore illegal. There was no question of mental abnormality but she was detained in this way for seven years until, at 24, NCCL successfully brought a case of *habeas corpus* in the High Court to obtain her freedom in February 1956. This case rested on the grounds that, far from having been neglected, the girl had been residing in a hospital and workhouse to which she had been sent.

Publicity surrounding the Rutty case again brought many more examples to light – 590 by the spring of 1956. Kathleen Bradley had been detained for more than 20 years following the failure of the local authority to find anyone to look after her at the age of 19 when she was recovering from an attack of rheumatic fever. She had been in the top stream at her school and had no record of delinquency but had been certified as mentally deficient and used as cheap labour. Despite the fact that many people had testified as to her sanity, it required a press campaign, questions in Parliament, two presentations to a Royal Commission and appeals to the Board of Control before she was finally released in late 1955.

The appointment of a Royal Commission was announced in late 1953. NCCL's long memorandum of evidence was submitted in 1954 and in March 1955 the Council's three witnesses (Allen, Robert George and Frank Haskell) gave oral evidence for a whole day, leading to the submission of supplementary information and a further oral examination in June 1955.[63] The NCCL's campaign continued with further public meetings. A leaflet advertising a Conference on Mental Deficiency Laws and Administration to be held in Beaver Hall on 30 June 1956 declared '...we invite you to come and help bring to a triumphant conclusion a campaign which has become a crusade for the weakest and most helpless section of the community, many of whom have from their childhood been deprived of their legal rights and subjected to many years of unwarranted detention, unjustifiable exploitation and inexcusable humiliation.'[64] The conference was attended by 200 delegates.

By that time NCCL had 850 mental deficiency cases on file, including 350 brought to their attention since the release of Kathleen Rutty. But it became clear that they were merely scratching the surface in terms of numbers, for parliamentary questions eventually revealed that as many as 5,732 similar cases existed. Attention became increasingly focused on the improper use of asylums for the criminally insane. This was illustrated by the case of Peter Whitehead, which showed that he had been held as a mental defective and transferred to Rampton at the age of 18, despite having no violent or criminal background. An independent examination showed him to be of average intelligence. NCCL successfully brought a writ of *habeas corpus* in 1956.

The Royal Commission reported in May 1957 and completely vindicated NCCL's campaign, presenting a savage attack on the existing mental health system. The resulting 1959 Mental Health Act abolished the 1913 Act and introduced Mental Health Review Tribunals which had to include at least one lay member. The new Act came fully into force in November 1960. NCCL established teams of volunteers to act for patients at these tribunals. Although 800 people had been released in 1957 and a further 1,000 in 1958, the need for vigilance and publicity continued. NCCL organised a further Conference on Mental Deficiency in Beaver Hall on 26 October 1957, attended by 150 delegates. New cases continued to come to light, including that of 'John', then 47, incarcarated since the age of three. Much of the credit for NCCL's enormous success in this area belonged to Frank Haskell, Head of the Mental Deficiency Department. He joined NCCL in 1946 but died on 24 February 1959.

Miscarriages of justice

The dominance of the mental health campaign could easily give the impression that by the 1950s NCCL had become practically a single issue pressure group. In truth, the range of interest and activities was as great as ever. The 1940s had seen the first of the celebrated miscarriages of justice cases which later came to dominate the British press in the 1980s.

In July 1949 the Court of Criminal Appeal quashed the conviction of John McGrath who, in October 1948, had been convicted for receiving stolen goods and had served nine months of his three year sentence. NCCL acted with the John McGrath Appeal Committee, led by Robert Mellish MP, in campaigning for his release, including sending a delegation to the Home Office in April 1949. The case of Timothy Evans, who was widely thought to have been wrongly hanged for the murder of a policeman in 1953, remains notorious, despite his eventual posthumous pardon. However, NCCL's greatest success in this area during the 1950s concerned a case of three wrongly convicted men which received extensive publicity in late 1955.[65]

The men had been convicted in January 1954 for an attack on a policeman to which someone else later confessed. The crime had occurred in Marlow, Buckinghamshire, on 16 October 1953 and the three men (Messrs Emery, Powers and Thompson) were arrested at 4am in a cafe in Brentford. Emery received a sentence of 10 years imprisonment, Thompson seven years and Powers four. Apart from the policeman, one prosecution witness had identified Thompson but without an identification parade. NCCL managed to find a witness who confirmed, as the men had claimed, that they were in Ashford, Middlesex, at the time of the attack. Furthermore, another man, then in prison, had confessed to the crime. The men were granted a Royal pardon in early 1956 and given financial compensation.

The McGrath case was subsequently featured in a television programme in 1956, with appearances by Robert Mellish and Elizabeth Allen, which resulted in many inquiries to NCCL. In November 1957 Allen again appeared on national television in order to state NCCL's opposition to the practice of telephone-tapping by the state.

Civil liberties in the British Empire and Commonwealth

From its earliest days NCCL's interests were much broader geographically than the British Isles, and this remained the case until the 1960s – in fact, for as long as Britain retained governmental or legal control of its imperial and Commonwealth possessions.

In its first year, NCCL helped a delegation from the Gold Coast (later Ghana) to meet MPs and gain publicity. In March 1938 NCCL organised a conference about Trinidad, following disturbances there in 1937, and this was followed the next year by a Conference on Labour Conditions in Kenya. In February 1941 a delegate conference on 'Civil Liberty in the Colonial Empire' was held at Conway Hall, Red Lion Square, chaired by A Creech Jones and attended by representatives from 235 organisations. NCCL's Overseas Sub-Committee produced a pamphlet, entitled *Civil Liberty and the Colonies,* in 1945, whilst in October of that year, NCCL organised a further conference on colonial affairs.

By the early 1950s attention had focused on Africa, and particularly South Africa. In June 1952 NCCL organised a protest meeting in London against repressive legislation there. This was followed by a conference in July attended by 130 delegates and a South Africa Protest Day on 30 September, which resulted in thousands of telegrams and letters of protest being delivered to South Africa House in London. Later, NCCL was again conspicuous in its support for the boycott of South Africa, so much so that, following the formation of the (fascist) British National Party in February 1960, the NCCL office windows were smashed by people throwing marbles at South African boycott posters.

5 Down, but not out

Despite the enormous interest generated by the mental health campaign during the 1950s, NCCL's overall position remained one of slow decline. In 1952 an urgent appeal for funds was necessary in order to stave off closure of the offices during the summer months. In the event, it proved possible to keep the offices open but only after a further reduction in staff numbers. By the end of the decade, the Council was badly affected by prolonged periods of staff illness and frequent office moves as leases expired.

These difficulties were compounded at times in small, but significant, ways. Telephones – or rather the lack of them – represented a constant source of irritation. Frank Haskell's home telephone was funded by the NCCL in recognition of the fact that it was used almost entirely in connection with confidential mental health cases. But in 1956 he was informed by the Post Office that he would have to share his line with a neighbour. The Post Office was unsympathetic to his plea for confidentiality and eventually removed the telephone completely. 'Much work that was previously done at week-ends and in the evenings cannot now be done,' recorded the 1956/57 *Annual Report,* 'so our activities are being seriously hampered.' By 1959, the NCCL office itself had only one telephone and many who rang had great difficulty in obtaining an answer.

The decade ended with DN Pritt's retirement from the EC. He had been a member for nearly 26 years. Elizabeth Allen's poor health seriously affected her work and she was made Honorary Secretary at her own request in 1958 before formally retiring in 1960. Barry Cox, author of *Civil Liberties in Britain* (published in 1975), observed in an interview in 1974 that 'Elizabeth Allen was an amazing woman. She was a very formidable lady, really powerful personality. She ran the thing for 20 years – she ran it too long; one of the reasons it was so moribund by the end of the fifties when Martin Ennals came was because she held on so long. But she did amazingly good work in that time – and had a very shrewd mind.'[66]

Allen remained on the EC for a couple of years but her worsening health (she bravely endured years of severe arthritis) eventually forced her to resign. She was succeeded as General Secretary by Martin Ennals, who had joined NCCL in 1959 as organising secretary after eight years working for UNESCO in Paris and the Middle East.

The early to mid-1960s probably represent NCCL's nadir. This is no reflection on the abilities and enthusiasm of Martin Ennals, who skilfully managed to prolong the life of an organisation which, in retrospect, appears to have been on the point of extinction. Malcolm Hurwitt, who served on the EC between the late 1950s and late 1980s, later wrote that Ennals was 'the most under-appreciated of General Secretaries'. When he took over, NCCL 'was stagnant and still suffering from the stigma of being a fellow-travelling Communist front.' Ennals revitalised it and provided the base upon which later General Secretaries were able to build.[67]

The situation in the early 1960s was certainly bleak. Individual membership fell below 2,000, although about two million people still had connections via affiliated bodies. John Tuchfeld, an EC member, later recalled that when he joined the Committee in 1962 (as a union nominee) there were fewer nominees than places, resulting in automatic election. This, he felt, reflected the organisation's lack of prestige at the time. More importantly, there were only three full-time members of staff.

In 1962 there also appeared to be only two major campaign issues – mental health and the administration of justice.[68] A paper on staffing prepared by Martin Ennals for the EC on 5 February 1964 noted that the full-time staff were Ennals himself, Mary Grigg and Otto Wolfgang (both clerical), plus a Mrs Stern who worked part-time, as did a Mrs Greenwood for the newly established Cobden Trust. There were also two unpaid volunteers in the Mental Health Department and four in the Legal Department.[69]

An inspection of issues of *Civil Liberty* for the period serves to emphasise the gloomy situation, for it had been reduced to a cheaply produced two-paged cyclo-styled foolscap newsletter, not dissimilar to the emergency issue of 1941 and not a document designed to inspire the reader. On the brighter side, the Cobden Trust (later to become the Civil Liberties Trust) was established in May 1963, essentially to take advantage of the British charity laws which allow tax advantages to registered charities and permit the receipt of donations from other charitable trusts. The original name derived from the statue of Richard Cobden which stood outside the offices at 4 Camden High Street and was noticed by Alan Paterson (an EC member, and Secretary of the Trust between 1963 and 1973) and deemed to be appropriate.[70]

The Trust's dual aims were first, to investigate the causes of injustice and, secondly, to help to educate people about their civil liberties. It has since undertaken a great deal of pioneering research and educational work in the field of civil liberties, particularly in areas such as women's rights and immigration law. In 1977 a series of leaflets on the theme of *Your rights and the police*, written in Chinese, Spanish, Urdu, Hindi, Gujerati, Bengali and Punjabi was issued. Other notable successes have included the publication of *Bail or Custody* (in 1971), which played an important part in the passage of the Bail Act, and *Civil Liberties and a Bill of Rights* (in 1976), which Lord Scarman described as 'the best piece of work on the subject yet published in this country.'[71]

On 10 December 1972, Ramsey Clark, the United States Attorney-General under President Johnson, gave the first of an annual series of Human Rights Day lectures organised by the Trust. Later lectures were given by Lord Scarman, Professor Stuart Hall, Jessica Mitford and Sir Keith Joseph and Tony Benn (in debate). The Trust also established and developed its own civil liberties library and played a key role in securing a permanent home for both itself and NCCL in 1981.

The colour bar, race relations and immigration

The exclusion of black people from certain jobs, public houses, clubs, rented flats, schools and hotels had long been of great concern to NCCL. In October 1939 the Council had drawn attention to several cases of civil defence workers refusing to work with black people and throughout the second world war highlighted the problems of black (especially American and Indian) servicemen in this country. In 1943 it had supported the case of the famous West Indian cricketer, Leary Constantine, against Imperial Hotel, London, when, having booked a room, Constantine was forced to move against his wishes to the Bedford Hotel.[72]

An important colour bar case in the late 1940s concerned incidents at Carrington House in Deptford. This 'common lodging house' usually held about 800 people including, from 1946, between 40 and 50 black immigrants. They were mainly from West Africa and had been directed to the hostel by the Colonial Office. These men experienced increasing antagonism from other residents and the local community and had difficulty securing jobs or being served in cafes and public houses. When, on the night of 18/19 July 1949, 14 of the men were arrested for 'affray' following a series of violent incidents, NCCL arranged their defence and secured the acquittal of most of them. Following further investigation by NCCL representatives, their complaints of race discrimination and colour bar restrictions were confirmed. A conference was subsequently organised at Goldsmiths College on 6 December 1949, leading to the establishment of a committee of local residents to help monitor the situation.[73]

The basic problem persisted, however. The 1951 *Annual Report* noted one public house in Paddington which had refused to serve black people on three occasions. The Hotel Proprietors' Act 1956 stated that keepers of hotels could not without lawful excuse refuse to provide refreshments to any traveller who appeared to be able to pay. And yet the *Annual Report* for 1958/59 noted the case of the Goring Hotel in London, where three black visitors from the United States of America, having made reservations, were then refused accommodation, solely on the basis of their colour.

Racism and the colour bar were particular concerns of the new General Secretary, Martin Ennals. A Colour Bar conference was held in November 1959 at Friends' Meeting House, with 210 delegates present. A related Conference on Anti-Semitism and Racial Incitement was held at the same venue in February 1960, attended by 121 people. This led to publication of the pamphlet *Anti-Semitism and Colour Bar – a Warning*, whilst Fenner Brockway's Racial Discrimination and Incitement Bill, supported by the NCCL, was introduced into the House of Commons for the 10th time in 1964, although Brockway unfortunately lost his seat at Eton and Slough in the general election later that year. Fortunately, others took up the cause championed by Brockway and the Race Relations Act 1965 eventually set up the Race Relations Board. Three further conferences on race relations were organised at Sheffield, Oxford and Leeds.

The imposition of ever stricter immigration controls also caused concern. The 1962 and 1968 Commonwealth Immigrants Acts greatly curtailed black immigration. Further controls were introduced under the 1971 Immigration Act and 1981 British Nationality Act. Eventually, in June 1968, NCCL organised an emergency 'Speak-out on race' meeting at the Friends' Meeting House in Euston Road, following Enoch Powell's 'rivers of blood' speech. This was one of the NCCL's most successful campaign issues during the 1960s.

Freedom of speech and assembly

Campaigns on the right to free speech and assembly were revived in the late 1950s and early 1960s in response to government and police behaviour towards the Campaign for Nuclear Disarmament (CND), which appears to have been treated as a threat to national security rather than a legitimate agency of protest.

Whilst CND had concentrated on peaceful demonstrations, the Committee of 100 was formed to organise protest by civil disobedience and, especially, the use of sit-down demonstrations to disrupt traffic. In London this led to mass arrests and the banning of public processions. In 1961 NCCL called for a public enquiry in a pamphlet entitled *Public Order and the Police*, expressing the fear that repressive measures, introduced by a government to prevent the disruption of law and order by an organisation trying to gain certain ends, could be used to prevent the advocacy of such ends and to suppress the organisers.

In September 1961 the Committee of 100 was refused permission to hold a rally in Trafalgar Square. In 1962 six organisers of the Committee were prosecuted and imprisoned under the Official Secrets Act, although no secrets were involved. That year also saw requests to use Trafalgar Square by the British National Party and Union Movement similarly refused.

NCCL regularly intervened in support of groups which were refused permission to demonstrate and closely monitored police behaviour during demonstrations throughout the 1960s. This was particularly important during the Grosvenor Square anti-Vietnam War protests beginning in 1965. However, the *Annual Report* for 1966 noted a change in police attitude, commenting that 'while the police themselves may sometimes infringe the rights of demonstrators, they are concerned that these rights should be publicly upheld, which is a long way from the situation that obtained 30 years ago.'

Administration of justice and the Challenor cases

Concern for fairness and honesty in the administration of justice was shown by the NCCL's support for individuals in numerous cases. But the system itself was also continually scrutinised for imperfections and the composition of juries was one area where action was clearly needed.

NCCL submitted a memorandum to the Departmental Committee on Jury Service at the Home Office, in October 1963. This noted that over half the adult population was excluded from jury service as a result of the property qualification laid down by the Juries Act of 1825. In reality, few people were judged by their peers. This applied especially to the poor, and to women, as there were many all-male juries. The NCCL's chief recommendation was that the property qualification should be repealed and all those on the electoral register should be eligible for jury service. In one case, reported in 1965, a convicted man claimed that the foreman of the jury was the taxi-driver who had driven him to court! NCCL succeeded in getting the case sent to the Court of Appeal.

In 1963 NCCL received some 321 applications for legal advice, of which 108 were against the police – including accusations of perjury, framing and brutality. Thirty-two complaints were concerned with judges' summing up and another 24 with the behaviour and performance of solicitors and counsel.

In 1964 500 complaints were dealt with, of which 150 were against the police, some of them particularly notorious.

The Challenor, or 'half-brick', cases attracted enormous public interest. They first came to light in 1963 when four young people, taking part in a demonstration, were accused of carrying offensive weapons in a public place. All maintained that the half-bricks in question had been planted on them at West End Central Police Station by Detective Sergeant Harold Gordon Challenor. At the hearings, where the defendants were supported by NCCL, all the charges were either dismissed or withdrawn and substantial compensation was paid by the police. Challenor was said to have been suffering from a mental breakdown and was subsequently investigated by the Director of Public Prosecutions.

The publicity associated with the case led to many other complaints against Challenor and some of his junior colleagues, followed by the release of a number of prisoners who had been serving long-term sentences. The resulting public inquiry led to the James report in August 1965 and, in the same year, Penguin published *The Challenor Case* by Mary Grigg, the Assistant Secretary of NCCL.

The Tony Smythe era

In 1966 Martin Ennals left to become Director of Amnesty International. By this time Malcolm Purdie had also retired as Chairman of the Executive Committee after 15 years and the office of President was revived in his honour. Ennals was succeeded as General Secretary by Tony Smythe, who had previously been General Secretary of War Resisters' International. His remarkably successful tenure at NCCL saw full-time staff numbers increase from three to 15, and membership figures rise from about 1,800 to 5,400.

In an interview in April 1974 Smythe explained that the two staff he inherited left quite soon afterwards and were replaced by 'rather splendid people'.[74] In early 1967 a bequest of £5,000 enabled a further appointment. Peter Burns was hired as Promotions Officer and helped to boost membership and secure additional funding from bodies such as the Rowntree Social Service Trust. Christine Jackson was also appointed as Research Officer, followed, most significantly, by Larry Grant as Legal Officer. Parliamentary lobbying was greatly helped by the development of the Parliamentary Civil Liberties Group under Eric Lubbock (later Lord Avebury) which had about 200 members at its peak.

When Smythe took over the major preoccupations of the Council were individual cases, usually to do with either the administration of justice, mental
health or immigration law. The period saw an increase in professionalism
and in membership for which Smythe was greatly helped by the fact that
there was a surge of interest in wider civil rights matters – with huge anti-
Vietnam demonstrations, student protests and great concern about immigration and racism. For NCCL the revival really began in 1968 – declared Human
Rights Year by the United Nations – with a major campaign on privacy and
a pamphlet entitled *Privacy Under Attack*. Many NCCL issues, then as now,
inevitably dealt with minorities and their (not always popular) interests. Privacy, on the other hand, affected everybody and was identified by Peter
Burns as an issue capable of attracting much interest and concern. Work in
the area of privacy continued when a Conference was organised in conjunction with the National Computing Centre in 1970 on 'The Data Bank Society'.
The NCCL also gave evidence to the Select Committee on Privacy, chaired
by Sir Kenneth Younger, which eventually reported in 1972.

New campaigns were undertaken in areas such as women's rights, and
the rights of travellers and gypsies. Section 127 of the Highways Act 1959
had made it an offence to camp on the highway, including the verges. In
one notorious case in late 1965, some gypsies in Orpington, coincidentally
the constituency of Eric Lubbock, were moved by representatives of the local
authority (the London Borough of Bromley) on to the public highway and
then summonsed for being on the public highway without excuse or authority. The archive also includes correspondence with the novelist Barbara
Cartland in May 1967 regarding the establishment of a Romany gypsy camp
at Mill Green, Hatfield, in Hertfordshire – known as 'Barbaraville'.[75] The Act
was eventually abolished in 1980 after a long campaign, to which NCCL con-
tributed the publication *On the Road* by Grattan Puxon in 1968. Also in that
year, Eric Lubbock steered the Caravan Sites Act through Parliament, although
initially its effects were very limited.

In January 1969 the Scottish Council for Civil Liberties was established
when the two local Scottish groups, based in Glasgow and Edinburgh, merged
to form a national organisation capable of reflecting the differences between
Scottish law and law elsewhere in the United Kingdom, and to counter the
relative neglect of Scottish issues by the national organisation. The SCCL became fully independent in early 1975.

Another related body, the Council for Academic Freedom and Democracy was launched at a meeting of academics in October 1970. It was effectively a standing commission of NCCL, although theoretically a separate organisation with its own offices and Executive Committee. Its activities initially centred on the work undertaken by Professor John Griffith at the London School of Economics, Ralph Miliband, John Westergaard and John Saville, and its first case was that of Anthony Arblaster at Manchester. Saville succeeded Griffith as Chairman in 1982 but, unfortunately, CAFD failed to last beyond the 1980s. Its surviving records – almost entirely case files – are now also held in the Brynmor Jones Library at the University of Hull.[76]

Reluctant servicemen

NCCL had a long interest in the rights of servicemen, dating from the end of World War Two. Since that time, the emphasis had shifted away from earlier concerns with the democratic rights of servicemen in general.

In 1951 a case came to light of a young man who, before the war, had been taken by his father to an Army Recruiting Centre where he had signed on as an apprentice for four years, to be followed by eight years in the army. Having signed on, there was little or no possiblity of release for those who realised they had made a mistake. Furthermore, official army service did not begin until the age of 18, so a boy of 14 or 15 could in fact be in service for 12 or even 16 years. Discharges could be purchased, for a sum, only during the first three months of service.

Public attention focused on the problem when there was a mass break-out of boy soldiers from the Royal Army Surgical Corps at Aldershot in April 1951, although nothing significant was done at the time. Servicemen were known to take desperate measures if their appeals for discharge failed, as they usually did. Such measures included desertion, feigned or real mental illness or homosexuality, breaking (or confessing to contraventions of) civil law, standing for Parliament, ostentatious adoption of left-wing views (for example, by ordering the *Daily Worker*), or even committing suicide.

Two weeks after Tony Smythe's arrival at NCCL, a reluctant serviceman came to the office. The case of Leading Engineer (Stoker) John Mayhew had first been brought to NCCL's attention in a letter from his mother in May 1966.[77] Mayhew had enlisted in the Royal Navy in 1957 at the age of 16. He soon realised that he had made a mistake and began to save the sum he was told was necessary to buy a discharge. He applied for this at the age of 18 only to find that he still had nine years to serve. Despite later being accepted for places at Bristol and Leicester Universities (in 1965 and 1966), for which he had the support of his Commanding Officer, his repeated applications for a discharge were turned down by the Admiralty. The massive campaign on his behalf was co-ordinated by NCCL and involved MPs, the press and television. A mention of the case on the David Frost television programme brought 20 new cases of frustrated servicemen to light, mainly from the Navy but some also from the Army and Air Force.

In 1970 NCCL published a report on the subject, *Civil Liberties and Service Recruitment*. Such publicity, pressure and further cases eventually led to the *Donaldson Report on Boy Entrants and Young Servicemen*, which appeared in 1970. Most of the Report's proposals were adopted by the new Conservative Government although on the crucial issue of discharge at the age of 18, a compromise was reached – men could decide at that age to leave the armed forces but would still have to wait until the age of 21 for the process to be completed.

6 Success in adversity: the 1970s and 1980s

By May 1971 the NCCL had a staff of 12. Its budget had increased from about £10,000 to around £30,000, and individual membership from 1,200 to 4,000, with 500 affiliated organisations. It also achieved a major publishing success in 1972 with *Civil Liberty: the NCCL Guide*, edited by Anna Coote and Lawrence Grant and published by Penguin Books. However, Tony Smythe left that year, eventually to become Director of MIND (the National Association for Mental Health).

His successor, Martin Loney, had been Director of Scientific Research for the World University in Geneva, and was a comparative stranger to Britain, having spent less than one year in the country since 1966. Loney was portrayed at the time (particularly in *The Times*) as very outspoken and notably left-wing. Some thought he was a Trotskyist, although he firmly denied this. Some suggested that his leadership, though loud, was uninspired and lacked new ideas. Unfortunately, his tenure coincided with a sudden fall in membership from 5,400 to 5,200 in 1973 and, more significantly, with the decision of a major funder, the Rowntree Social Service Trust, to reduce its annual contribution from £10,500 to a proposed £2,000 in 1976.

Some staff felt Loney was basically doing a good job and wanted him to stay. Others, including certain members of the EC – at least one of whom was particularly upset by Loney's apparent support for the policy of internment in Northern Ireland – were unimpressed. Loney was dismissed on 6 June 1974 after only 17 months in the post. The bitter public wrangle which followed in the press did no credit to the NCCL at a time when the severe effects of the great wage and price inflation of the 1970s were beginning to bite. Professor Laurie Taylor and Dr Stanley Cohen (both of the Department of Sociology at the University of York) were particularly critical of the way in which Loney had been treated, pointing out in an article in *The Guardian* on 15 June 1974 that NCCL would have been quick to condemn such behaviour elsewhere.

At least one major advance during the Loney period was the establishment of the Women's Rights Sub-Committee in 1973. In September 1973 Patricia Hewitt, previously at Age Concern, was appointed Women's Rights Officer. This quickly led, in February 1974, to a conference on women, trade unions and work, and an associated pamphlet entitled *Danger: Women at Work*. Also, a women's rights page became a regular feature of *Civil Liberty*.

Another success was the 'foreign husbands' campaign. This focused attention on the fact that, in getting married, women took on the nationality of their husbands. The campaign, conducted in collaboration with the Equal Opportunities Commission and with the backing of many MPs, eventually led to a Private Member's Bill, put forward by Jill Knight, seeking to give children the right to acquire the nationality of their mothers. Whilst this was lost, in February 1979 the Home Secretary, Merlyn Rees, announced that in future he would use his discretionary power to enable children born in the United Kingdom to British women who were married to foreign men to be registered as British citizens.

Northern Ireland

The NCCL's long involvement in Northern Ireland began with its investigation in the 1930s into the operation of the Special Powers Acts of 1922 and 1933. In March 1965 NCCL organised a Conference on Northern Ireland in London about allegations of discrimination against Roman Catholics and the need for reform of the electoral system. It was chaired by Eric Lubbock, Chair of the Parliamentary Civil Liberties Group. NCCL also helped to set up the Northern Ireland Civil Rights Association in 1967.

The effects of the onset of the 'troubles', followed by the introduction of the British Army in place of police in Belfast in August 1969, the rise of the Provisional IRA in 1970/71 and the temporary introduction of internment in August 1971, presaged a turn for the worse. On 30 January 1972 a Civil Rights march in Londonderry resulted in 13 deaths – the second 'Bloody Sunday'. NCCL subsequently obtained 600 statements from witnesses and provided this evidence to Sam Dash (of the International League for the Rights of Man) who in his report, *Justice Denied*, found that the army had been criminally reckless.[78] The Emergency Powers Act was replaced by the Special Powers Act in 1973, followed, in 1974, by direct rule (with William Whitelaw as the first Northern Ireland Secretary), and by the Prevention of Terrorism (Temporary Provisions) Act. All these were strenuously opposed by NCCL. The extreme dangers of the situation were made clear in April 1974 when a Special Branch informer, Kenneth Lennon, was found dead in a ditch in Surrey. Forty-eight hours earlier he had spent six hours giving a statement about his underground activities to NCCL's Legal Officer, Larry Grant.[79]

Financial problems

Patricia Hewitt took over as acting General Secretary following the sudden departure of Martin Loney. A Special General Meeting, called by members disturbed by the dismissal of Loney, was held in September 1974 but simply confirmed the original decision. Hewitt was formally appointed General Secretary in December that year.

NCCL was badly hit by the high inflation which characterised much of the 1970s and the resulting financial crisis led to the removal of five posts. Such measures were needed despite the fact that an internal survey and report had assessed the workloads of every member of office staff and found that Hewitt alone worked an average 67 hours a week.[80] In late 1974 there were 16 full-time staff. By 1978 this had been reduced to nine full-time and four part-time, with two volunteers and a placement student. Operations were also complicated by a very high staff turnover. A special appeal in December 1976 saved a further three threatened posts. By December 1977 there were 4,765 members and 800 affiliates.

Despite the reductions in staff, the continued effects of wage inflation actually increased staff costs in 1976. Furthermore, monies from grants by charitable trusts, which had accounted for 25 per cent of all income in 1973, fell to just four per cent in 1976. In 1976/77 income was £3,792 less than expenditure and the following year £9,000 less – NCCL was on the verge of bankruptcy. Another appeal was launched, producing £17,000.

Lesbian and gay rights

Gay rights was an increasing area of activity from the mid-1970s. NCCL's Gay Rights Committee was formed in 1974, along with the appointment of a Gay Rights Organiser, Nettie Pollard, and the launch of its Gay Rights Campaign. During this period NCCL published the results of two surveys into job discrimination and fought important test cases. In 1975 NCCL established the right of a lesbian midwife to become a health visitor, by appealing to a local Health Authority on behalf of Veronica Pickles. It was the first non-gay organisation to take up lesbian and gay rights as a priority and the first to organise a conference on the topic. The Homosexual Freedom conference in London had speakers on a variety of aspects of lesbian and gay oppression and attracted a wide-ranging audience. In the 1970s NCCL became known as the best organisation to go to for support of lesbian and gay issues.

In 1980 a generous donation from an individual supporter enabled the appointment of a full-time Gay Rights Officer (initially Barry Prothero), although money for this post ran out in 1983, despite a grant from the Greater London Council for the Gay Community Policing Project. Concern about official harassment was heightened when, on 10 April 1984, Customs and Excise officers confiscated 800 volumes – one-third of the stock – of the Gay's the Word Bookshop in London, along with company records. The bookshop had opened in 1979, with support from the GLC, amongst others. NCCL's Annual General Meeting carried a motion in support of the shop and called for a review of Customs' powers to seize and destroy imported books. NCCL also agreed to act as the bookshop's solicitors. All charges were eventually dropped and the books were returned in June 1986. Two years later, the NCCL jointly campaigned with other organisations against Clause 28 of the Local Government Bill which prohibited the 'promotion of homosexuality' by local authorities.

New campaigns

Under Patricia Hewitt's guidance, campaigning branched out into several new areas, such as consumer credit, sex discrimination, gay rights, privacy and freedom of information. Activity in areas such as race relations, the role of the police and Northern Ireland continued as before. A particular interest in the late 1970s was penal reform and casework involving prisoners and miscarriages of justice. But one of NCCL's greatest publicity successes at this time was in the area of personal privacy.

The firm of Tracing Services Ltd, which went into liquidation in 1974, had specialised in compiling confidential private financial information on individuals. Two of its directors had been convicted, in February 1969, of effecting a public mischief by using fraudulent means and dishonest devices to obtain information. Members of the company had impersonated doctors, police officers, Inland Revenue officials and others. Information on the company was included in the NCCL's evidence to the Younger Committee on Privacy. In January 1975 NCCL bought three million credit-rating files from Konfax Limited after they had been offered for sale in the *Evening Standard* on 28 January. A further two million files, which were to have been sold to a Scottish credit-rating agency, were also purchased. One penny was paid for the files, which were promptly destroyed. NCCL later gave evidence to the Lindop Data Protection Committee in 1977 (which reported in 1978) and in the same year launched a Right to Know campaign.[81]

The decade ended with the tragic death of a protester. The social and political disruptions of the late 1970s had, perhaps inevitably, included renewed efforts by the extreme right to gain support, or at least attention. On 23 April 1979 a National Front meeting at Southall, in the middle of Britain's largest Asian community, held during the general election campaign, was countered by an anti-fascist protest. The death of Blair Peach during the demonstration resulted in calls for a public enquiry, which were refused by the Labour Home Secretary, Merlyn Rees and his Conservative successor after the election, William Whitelaw. Representatives of the local community approached NCCL, which set up its own inquiry under Professor Michael Dummett of New College, Oxford, in July 1979. The report, published in April 1980, strongly criticised the behaviour of both demonstrators and police. A delegation led by Professor Dummett met Whitelaw in July 1980 but the Home Secretary still refused to allow a public inquiry.[82]

Into the 1980s and firmly into Europe

The policies of successive Conservative Governments since 1979, whilst allegedly intended to 'roll back' the frontiers of the state in order to extend personal choice, in practice appeared to strengthen the hands of the central authority and remove power from potential sources of opposition. Legislation affecting trade unions and their members, local government (including its abolition, in some places), local taxation, security and immigration control was introduced. One commentator, summarising the decade, wrote, 'The Government has produced almost a state of peacetime emergency.'[83] Not surprisingly, the period witnessed a massive increase in workload for the Council in all areas of its activity.

One of the most important developments during the 1980s, partly a response to these anti-libertarian trends, was the use of European institutions and legislation on behalf of British citizens inadequately served by their own legal and governmental systems. The European Convention on Human Rights, ratified by the United Kingdom as an international treaty as long ago as 1951, became an important weapon with which the British Government could be both embarrassed and, on occasion, forced to compensate the victims of injustice. The ECHR guarantees such basic rights as freedom of religion, the right to privacy and the right to a fair trial, though the failings of the ECHR itself were recognised and NCCL investigated ways in which it could be improved. *An Effective Remedy? – a Review of the Procedure of the ECHR* appeared in 1981 and in November that year NCCL hosted a seminar on the topic for interested parties at the Royal Commonwealth Society in London.

But it was NCCL's support of individual cases, using the European Convention, which proved most effective and newsworthy. Since 1966 it had been possible for individual complainants to go to the European Commission of Human Rights at Strasbourg, and thence to either the European Court or the Council of Ministers. In most years, certainly in the 1980s, the largest number of complaints from any one country came from British citizens. In August 1982, NCCL supported an application to the Commission by Kathleen Stewart after she had failed to obtain redress in Belfast High Court for the death of her 13 year-old son – hit by a plastic bullet in October 1976. This case was the first to challenge the use of plastic bullets under international human rights law.

NCCL also lodged a series of test cases with the European Commission in 1982, in conjunction with the Joint Council for the Welfare of Immigrants, as part of a continuing campaign against immigration rules affecting foreign husbands and fiancés. Three such cases were declared admissable after a hearing at Strasbourg in May 1982. This centred on the claim that British immigration rules denied the right to marry and establish a family and did so in a way that discriminated on the grounds of sex and race. Other cases over the years concerned employment rights – particularly in relation to equal pay for women, sexual harassment, trade union membership and the rights of part-time workers – abolition of corporal punishment in state schools, rights for homosexuals in Northern Ireland and the extension of prisoners' rights. A long-standing (and continuing) campaign by NCCL has been the demand to incorporate the ECHR into European law so that individuals may pursue cases in their home countries rather than at Strasbourg.

The 1980s also produced several instances where the British legal system itself was made to look inept. An example of this occurred in 1980 following the prosecution of the Legal Officer, Harriet Harman, for contempt of Court. Harman had defended Michael Williams in the High Court in an action concerning the Home Office's Prison Control Units, of which he had been the first inmate. Copies of documents obtained for the defence, having been used and even read out in open Court, were shown to *The Guardian* and used in a major article. The Williams case was lost, Harman was found guilty of contempt of court and this decision was narrowly upheld by the Court of Appeal (under Lord Denning) in November 1981.[84] Her case went to the House of Lords where she lost, and then to the ECHR, where she won, eventually forcing the Government to amend the law as a result.

In 1981, together with the Cobden Trust, NCCL purchased much-needed permanent premises at 21-23 Tabard Street in south east London for about

SIXTY YEARS IN ILLUSTRATIONS

the
30s

1   Ronald Kidd, founder of the NCCL, in the late 1930s

Leaflet issued by the first NCCL, December 1918

Circular letter issued by Ronald Kidd,
1 February 1934

Birthplace of the NCCL, St Martin-in-the-Fields
Church in central London [Brian Dyson]

THE NATIONAL COUNCIL FOR CIVIL LIBERTIES

CONSTITUTION

1. This Society shall be called the National Council for Civil Liberties.

2. STATEMENT OF AIMS.—The aims of the Council shall be to assist in the maintenance of the hard-won rights of citizens— especially freedom of speech, press and assembly—from all infringement by executive or judicial authority contrary to due process of law, or by the tendency of governmental and other agencies to use their powers at the expense of the precarious liberties for which citizens of this country have fought. Wherever the Executive Committee of the Council may so decide, the Council shall aid in advancing measures for the recovery and enlargement of these liberties and for the reform of existing relevant legislation. The Council shall further these aims by vigilant observation, Press activity, legal advice, organised protest, and other appropriate means.

3. The Council shall be non-party and undenominational.

4. The Council shall consist of an Executive Co[...] more than 24 members, and of Associate Memb[...] Members shall pay a minimum annual subscription [...] and shall declare their adhesion to the above sta[...] The Executive Committee shall be elected by b[...] of one year's standing, from among nominees [...] group of ten such members, or by the Exe[...] One-third of the Executive Committee, in or[...] election, shall retire annually, but shall be elig[...] Nominations may be submitted at any time w[...] the Annual Meeting.

2

GREAT MASS
DEMONSTRATION
AGAINST THE
SEDITION BILL

Sunday, June 24, 1934

UNDER THE AUSPICES OF

The London Trades Council
AND
The Council for Civil Liberties.

OFFICIAL PROGRAMME
PRICE - 1d.

5   Hunger marchers in Hyde Park, 25 February 1934
    [Hulton-Deutsch Picture Library]

6   Sylvia Crowther-Smith, NCCL's first Assistant
    General Secretary [Sylvia Scaffardi]

7   The first constitution of the NCCL from
    the Annual Report of 1934/35

8   Cover of anti-Sedition Bill demonstration
    programme, 24 June 1934

9   EM Forster, NCCL's first President,
     in 1938 [National Portrait Gallery]

10   The anti-sedition cartoon by Low
     as it appeared in *The Sedition Bill
     Explained*, by W Ivor Jennings,
     in October 1934

9

10

NURSEMAIDS IN THE PARK— *NEW STYLE.*

34-94
the
30s

11

12

11   Baton charge by mounted police in Thurloe Square,
     London, 22 March 1936

12   Ronald Kidd delivers the Harworth Colliery petition,
     containing more than 250,000 signatures, to the
     Home Office on 8 September 1937

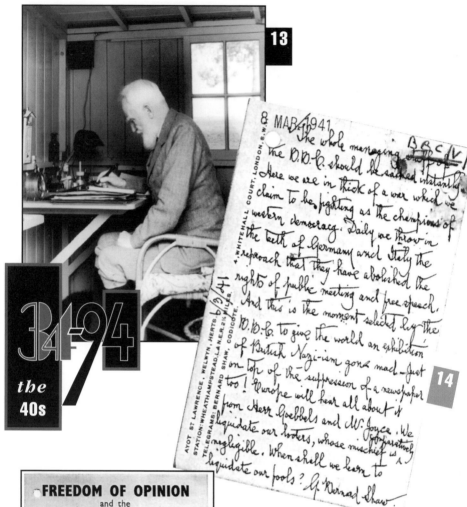

13

8 MAR 1941

The whole managing staff of the B.B.C. should be sacked instantly. Here we are in the thick of a war which we claim to be fighting as the champions of western democracy. Daily we throw in the teeth of Germany and Italy the reproach that they have abolished the right of public meeting and free speech. And this is the moment selected by the B.B.C. to give the world an exhibition of British Nazi-ism gone mad—just on top of the suppression of a newspaper too! Europe will hear all about it from Herr Goebbels and Mr. Joyce. We liquidate our traitors, whose mischief is comparatively negligible. When shall we learn to liquidate our fools? G. Bernard Shaw.

4, WHITEHALL COURT, LONDON, S.W.
STATION: WHEATHAMPSTEAD, L.N.E.R. 2¼ MILES.
TELEGRAMS: BERNARD SHAW, CODICOTE.
AYOT ST. LAWRENCE, WELWYN, HERTS. 6/3/41

FREEDOM OF OPINION
and the
B.B.C.

E. M. FORSTER
MICHAEL REDGRAVE
BEATRIX LEHMANN
PHIL CARDEW
THE ARCHDEACON OF
WESTMINSTER
(CANON F. LEWIS DONALDSON)

PROTEST MEETING
CONWAY HALL
RED LION SQUARE, LONDON, W.C.1

Monday, March 17th, 6 p.m.
Convened by the
NATIONAL COUNCIL FOR CIVIL LIBERTIES
37, Great James Street, London, W.C.1 (Holborn 9671)
FREE ADMISSION

Vail & Co., Ltd., E.C.1

13 George Bernard Shaw, NCCL member, in 1937 [National Portrait Gallery]

14 Postcard from George Bernard Shaw to Ronald Kidd about BBC censorship, 6 March 1941 [Society of Authors]

15 Poster advertising a protest meeting against the BBC, 17 March 1941

16 Delegates at a conference on 'Civil Liberty and the Defeat of Fascism', Central Hall, Westminster, 24 August 1940

17 Harold Laski's letter of resignation, over Communist influence, 13 May 1941

18 HW Nevinson, NCCL President 1936-1941, seen here in 1940

19 Cover of the NCCL's journal, Civil Liberty Vol.4, No.6, December 1943

VOL. 4 NO. 6 | DECEMBER 1943   TWOPENCE

CIVIL LIBERTY

JOURNAL OF THE NATIONAL COUNCIL FOR CIVIL LIBERTIES
11a KINGS ROAD, LONDON S.W.3   SLOane 5279

Page 1: The Release of Sir Oswald and Lady Mosley; Regulation 18 B;
page 2: "It shall not happen here"; page 3: Detention Camps; page 4:
Agents provocateur

THE RELEASE OF SIR OSWALD AND LADY MOSLEY

THE HOME SECRETARY'S ANNOUNCEMENT OF HIS INTENTION TO RELEASE SIR OSWALD AND LADY Mosley, followed by the actual release, has raised a storm of protest throughout the country. Protests by powerful Trade Unions, by factory workers, by office workers, by individuals, have poured in to the Home Office and to No. 10 Downing Street. The collection of signatures to petitions has been made in the street.

The following resolution, which was adopted by the Executive Committee of the N.C.C.L. at an emergency meeting on 19th November, was sent to the Prime Minister and the Home Secretary. It was reported in the B.B.C. News Bulletins at 6.0 p.m. and 9.0 p.m. on the same day, and was quoted extensively in the Press:—

"The National Council for Civil Liberties deplores the decision to release Sir Oswald and Lady Mosley. The release at this time of the avowed leader of British Fascism can only encourage Fascism and Anti-Semitism.

Whatever pretext may be advanced, this step must create the most profound disquiet in the minds of all those who are fighting or working against Fascism, and who know that its survival, either in this country or abroad, threatens all our civil liberties."

This journal goes to Press before Parliament has been able to debate the matter, but neither Parliament nor the Government can be in any doubt as to the feelings of the people of this country who, in the midst of the war they are waging against Fascism, resent the release of the man who is the symbol of British Fascism—the enemy of civil liberty.

REGULATION 18b

THE RELEASE OF SIR OSWALD AND LADY MOSLEY HAS LED TO CONSIDERABLE DISCUSSION ON Defence Regulation 18B in some quarters.

Readers may like to be reminded of the statement on Regulation 18B which was adopted by the Executive Committee of the N.C.C.L. at its meeting in July, 1942, and which was published in the July-August, 1942, issue of "Civil Liberty." The following are relevant extracts from the statement:—

"Just as the Fascist tactic of organising a 'Fifth Column' among the nationals of the countries with which it is at war is new to us, so is the principle of the detention without trial of suspected people under Defence Regulation 18B. This Regulation cuts right across that deep-rooted traditional principle of British justice that no one shall be imprisoned without being brought to trial.

We recognise the need for restrictive legislation in war-time, but it is our duty to ensure that that legislation is only used for the purposes of democracy and is not misused.

Clearly, it would have grave consequences for national security and the larger civil liberties of the rest of the country if Fascists, Fascist sympathisers or those of dubious loyalty were allowed to be free to conduct activities against the interests of the people. Such activities, if successful, might lead to the establishment of Fascism and the abolition of all civil liberties in this country. In any case, the measures which would have to be taken to combat them would bear heavily upon

Contd. page 2.   1

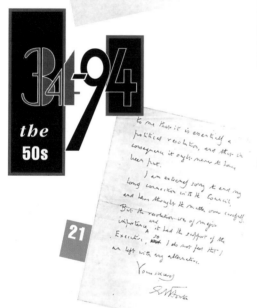

the
50s

20 Cover of *Freedom for the Forces* pamphlet, 1947

21 EM Forster's letter of resignation, 30 April 1948
    [King's College, Cambridge]

22 Cover of *50,000 Outside the Law,* pamphlet on the treatment of mental health patients, 1951

23 Frank Haskell, responsible for
    ground-breaking mental health
    work between 1947 and 1959

24 Poster to promote an anti-race
    discrimination meeting,
    29 September 1958

25 Elizabeth Acland Allen, NCCL
    General Secretary, 1941-1960

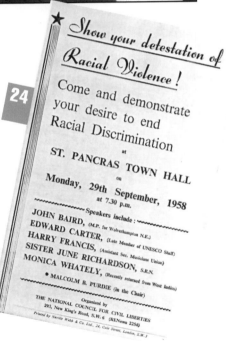

★ Show your detestation of
Racial Violence !

Come and demonstrate
your desire to end
Racial Discrimination

at

ST. PANCRAS TOWN HALL

on

Monday, 29th September, 1958

at 7.30 p.m.

Speakers include :

JOHN BAIRD, (M.P. for Wolverhampton N.E.)
EDWARD CARTER, (Late Member of UNESCO Staff)
HARRY FRANCIS, (Assistant Sec. Musicians Union)
SISTER JUNE RICHARDSON, S.R.N.
MONICA WHATELY, (Recently returned from West Indies)

● MALCOLM B. PURDIE (in the Chair)

Organised by
THE NATIONAL COUNCIL FOR CIVIL LIBERTIES
293, New King's Road, S.W. 6   (RENown 2254)

Printed by Neville Webb & Co. Ltd., 24, Cole Street, London, S.W.1

34-94
the
50s

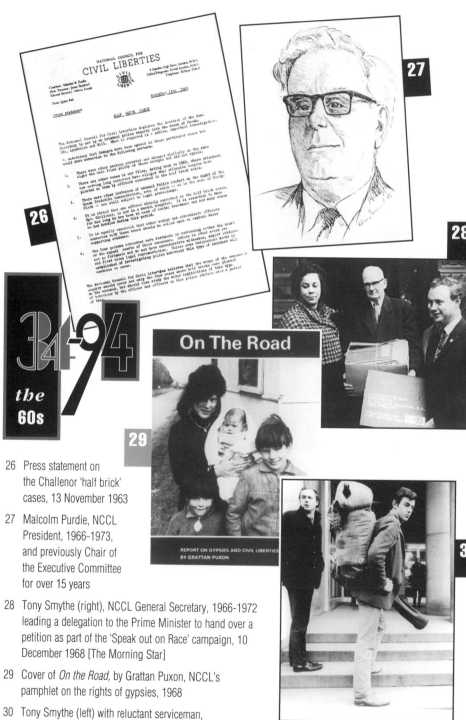

the 60s

26 Press statement on
the Challenor 'half brick'
cases, 13 November 1963

27 Malcolm Purdie, NCCL
President, 1966-1973,
and previously Chair of
the Executive Committee
for over 15 years

28 Tony Smythe (right), NCCL General Secretary, 1966-1972
leading a delegation to the Prime Minister to hand over a
petition as part of the 'Speak out on Race' campaign, 10
December 1968 [The Morning Star]

29 Cover of *On the Road*, by Grattan Puxon, NCCL's
pamphlet on the rights of gypsies, 1968

30 Tony Smythe (left) with reluctant serviceman,
Corporal Michael Hall, as he gives himself up at the Ministry of Defence, 1968 [The Daily Telegraph]

31 Gay's the Word bookshop,
central London, which was
raided by Customs and
Excise officers in 1984

32 Patricia Hewitt, NCCL
General Secretary 1974–
1983, with some of the five
million personal files bought
from Konfax for one penny
in 1975

34-94

the
70s

&
the
80s

33 Four General Secretaries
left to right: Larry Gostin,
Tony Smythe, Patricia Hewitt
and Martin Ennals at the Golden
Jubilee celebrations in February
1984 [Andrew Wiard]

34 An NCCL observer at a CND protest in London, 9 June 1984 [John Harris/International Freelance Library]

35 NCCL members vote at the AGM, 28 April 1985 [Stefano Cagnoni, Report]

36 Police confront a miners' picket at Orgreave Colliery, Yorkshire, 18 June 1984 [John Harris/International Freelance Library]

the
80s

35

36

37 The NCCL re-launch as Liberty, on 24 January 1989. Left to right:
    Rabbi Julia Neuberger, Richard Shepherd MP, Sarah Spencer, NCCL General Secretary 1985-1989,
    Robin Cook MP and Harold Pinter, playwright [Andrew Moore/Reflex Picture Agency]

38 Liberty's guide book to Section 28 and all its implications

39 Poster protesting against the threat to privacy implications of the poll tax in the late 1980s

40 Cover of Liberty's Annual Review 1989

41 Press conference held 24 April 1990 after ruling that MI5 surveillance of Harriet Harman (centre) and Patricia Hewitt (right) had breached European human rights law. They are accompanied here by General Secretary Andrew Puddephatt (left). [Martin Keene/Press Association]

42 *A People's Charter*, Liberty's Bill of Rights published in 1992

43 Poster as part of the campaign for a Bill of Rights

44 Andrew Puddephatt, General Secretary of Liberty, 1989 to date

45 Logo for Justice in Crisis
    campaign, launched in 1991

46 Actress Zoë Wanamaker signs Liberty's Charter
    for Justice on Justice Day 1992 [John Harris]

47 Covers of the first three of the Human Rights
    Convention reports, published in 1993

48 The Burnsall Strikers, awarded the Martin Ennals
    Civil Liberties award in December 1993 [Mark Salmon]

*All illustrations c/o the
Liberty Archive, Brynmor Jones
Library, Hull University, except
where otherwise indicated.*

34-94

civil
liberties
trust

£120,000. These were first occupied in November of that year, and became the eighth address the NCCL had had since 1948, other residencies having lasted between a decade and a few months. To ensure long-term continuity the trustees of the Cobden Trust became shareholders and directors of the company which acquired the property. Coincidentally, perhaps, this major success was followed by a large financial deficit in 1981/82, prompting a reduction in the frequency of *Rights* (formerly *Civil Liberty*), with the first issue of 1982 limited to just four pages and accompanied by an appeal for funds.

Having been adopted as a Labour Party Parliamentary candidate, and with a general election imminent, Patricia Hewitt announced her impending resignation at the Annual General Meeting in the summer of 1983, saying 'We are now a permanent part of the political and legal life of this country. . . NCCL is too important to be identified with one individual or one group. We hold NCCL in trust for the next generation – and both it, and the cause of civil liberties, deserve the best that we can give.'[85] She had certainly become one of the country's best known campaigners. The period after her departure was a time when the NCCL needed to be at peak effectiveness. Sadly, despite hard work and some notable successes, this was not always the case and attentions were all too frequently focused on internal disputes.

Larry Gostin and the Golden Jubilee 'Liberty' Campaign

Patricia Hewitt's successor was Dr Larry Gostin, a member of the New York bar and a civil rights campaigner in the United States since the 1960s. He had a particular interest in mental health and, after coming to Britain in 1974 as a Fulbright Fellow, joined Tony Smythe at MIND as Legal Officer. Two-thirds of the Mental Health (Amendment) Act of 1982 was based upon his book, *A Human Condition*.[86] A distinguished academic, he became Visiting Fellow in Law and Psychiatry at Oxford University Centre for Criminological Research prior to his appointment at NCCL.

His arrival was followed almost immediately by celebrations to mark the golden jubilee of NCCL's foundation. On 22 February 1984 a letter under the heading 'The Golden Age of Liberty', signed by Lord Avebury, Lord Brockway, Michael Foot, Glenda Jackson, EP Thompson, Larry Gostin and others, was published in *The Guardian*, recollecting an equivalent letter in 1934. It noted how, in some respects, things had changed very little – especially in relation to Northern Ireland and the Government's reliance on themes such as 'law and order' and 'national security' to justify what appeared to be a sustained attack on the liberties of the citizen. The letter announced a re-launch of the Liberty campaign in the form of a 'Charter of Civil Rights and Liberties', which stated:

> As our world changes, so will the concerns of the NCCL; but the need for a Council to safeguard civil liberties will be as pressing in 50 years time as it is now, and was in 1934.

The publication of the Charter in the *Guardian* as a full page advertisement paid for by its 1300 signatories resulted in over 1000 new members. The campaign in 1984 also saw the re-establishment of an All-Party Parliamentary Civil Liberties Group, with Conservative, Labour and Liberal members.

Rent asunder: GCHQ, advice policy, and the miners' strike

The mid-1980s revealed deep divisions in the leadership and membership of NCCL over a number of otherwise unrelated matters.

The Government's ban on trade union membership at its secret communications base in Cheltenham caused considerable upset both within the trade union movement and the membership of NCCL. Then, as now, there was overwhelming support within NCCL for the right to belong to an independent trade union. However, in December 1984, John Bennett, a member of the EC who described himself as 'on the right', resigned, arguing that NCCL was influenced in its policy by its heavy reliance on union funding, and was missing what he thought was the real issue at Cheltenham – namely, the use of lie detectors to ascertain the political loyalties of employees. He also noted NCCL's additional reliance on funding from the Greater London Council and appealed for the election of a more broadly-based Executive Committee to help Larry Gostin.[87] It is worth noting that in 1984/85 the GLC in fact provided grants totalling £83,041 – nearly one-third of total income. This money was doubtless very welcome but such reliance on one source was potentially extremely dangerous, as was demonstrated shortly afterwards when the GLC was abolished.

Successive AGMs, in April 1984 and April 1985, revealed additional major policy differences within the membership and leadership of NCCL, differences which came close to destroying the organisation's credibility. Two main issues were dominant – advice policy and the miners' dispute.

In 1984 NCCL had given advice to Joseph Pearce, a leading member of the National Front and editor of its magazine, *Bulldog*, whose home had been raided and ransacked by the police. In another incident, help was sought by NF members whose bus had been detained by the police and then turned back whilst on the way to an anti-IRA march. In the same year, as Larry Gostin later pointed out, NCCL also campaigned on behalf of Kent miners who had been stopped whilst travelling to a picket outside their own region. On 24 March 1984, the *Guardian* published a story about advice given by NCCL staff to members of the NF and a major row broke out. Larry Gostin was supported in his decision to give advice to NF members by the EC but this decision was overruled by the AGM at City University in April. A resolution was passed stating that 'NCCL should not knowingly aid organisations or individuals representing organisations whose primary objectives are opposed to civil liberties within a multi-racial society.'

According to Larry Gostin, during the following year the EC's interpretation of the AGM's decisions effectively prevented NCCL staff from giving advice to individuals with 'well-known racist views', regardless of whether they belonged to a racist organisation. At the 1985 AGM Gostin and others fought for their view. 'It should not be our place,' he said, 'to reserve our aid [from] those we disapprove of.' In fact this AGM modified advice policy by making a distinction between individuals and organisations, supporting the principle that advice and, where appropriate, assistance, should be given to individuals regardless of their beliefs. Nevertheless, applications by known members of the NF to join NCCL in 1985 were rejected by the EC in order to prevent a suspected infiltration of the organisation. A new application form asked individuals to sign a clause supporting NCCL's aims and objectives. This was something which people with such views could not genuinely do. One member – an Englishman resident in the United States, who had links with the Ku Klux Klan – was formally expelled on these grounds. The AGM's deliberations were complicated by the case of an NF student at North London Polytechnic, a case which prompted it to uphold 'the principle that no person should be excluded from access to education or other public service on the grounds of political or other opinion.'

A second major source of dispute involved the miners' strike. The 1984 AGM had decided to set up an independent inquiry into the policing of the strike, chaired by Professor Peter Wallington of Lancaster University. Whether the AGM wanted an inquiry independent of the government, or of NCCL itself, remains a subject of debate. The Inquiry's remit was 'To inquire into and thereby establish the fullest possible account and the civil liberties implications of the role of the police, the police authorities and the events arising from and relating to the NUM dispute, which began in March 1984.'

Its interim report, *Civil Liberties and the Miners' Dispute*, was published later that year. This pointed out that, in order to assess the behaviour of the police, it was necessary also to consider that of the strikers. As an example, it was noted that picketing of the homes of non-striking miners constituted a challenge to the civil liberties of the families of such men. Overall, the report was highly critical of the policing of the strike and supported the collective right to strike and picket.

The majority of the EC, meeting on 28 February 1985, considered that the inquiry team had gone well beyond its brief and passed a motion 'regretting' the report as 'unnecessarily damaging to the miners' cause'. The AGM in April 1985 supported the EC's view and defeated a motion that 'only considerations of civil liberties are relevant to NCCL and that it is improper for it to take sides in an industrial dispute.' Generally, however, the AGM accepted the interim report, with the exception of one key sentence – 'Freedom not to take part in a strike is as much a fundamental right as the right to strike.' This rejection was on the grounds that such a principle 'undermines the collective rights of others, and cannot be supported as a fundamental freedom.' The members of the inquiry team immediately decided that they could not continue under the auspices of the NCCL but would complete their work as private individuals.[88] In a letter published in *Civil Liberty*, Professor Wallington explained, 'We would all deeply regret that the internal political disputes within NCCL should prevent the publication of a report of major importance in the defence of civil liberties.'[89]

The members of the inquiry team included Larry Gostin and, at the first EC meeting after the AGM, Gostin resigned, claiming that NCCL had been taken over by the left. These public splits did great damage to NCCL's reputation and the internal dispute rumbled on for some time.

Money problems and reorganisation

Larry Gostin was replaced by Sarah Spencer. Although only 32 years old, she had been Director of the Cobden Trust (which she had first joined as Research Officer), had edited the NCCL's journal for six years and had published widely on civil rights issues.

The problems confronting her were considerable and did not just relate to the after-effects of the 1985 AGM and Gostin's departure. The demise of the GLC at the end of March 1986 was a major financial blow. The decision of the House of Lords in April to prevent the GLC from giving transitional funding to voluntary organisations after its abolition resulted in a major NCCL cash crisis and another appeal for £30,000 to stave off cuts in work and threatened redundancies. Three staff on temporary GLC-funded projects were lost. Eventually the appeal raised some £50,000. As was by now customary at such times, *Civil Liberty* saw its frequency reduced from eight to six issues annually as an economy measure.

Sarah Spencer and her colleagues set to work on revitalising the organisation. NCCL staffing was restructured, with a team of management consultants introduced in July 1987. A thorough management re-organisation took place in July 1988. Four departments were established: Legal & Campaigning; Promotion; Finance & Administration; and Women's Rights. Each had a team leader who, together with the General Secretary, formed a management team. There remained a Director of the Cobden Trust, renamed the Civil Liberties Trust in 1987, but overall responsibilty rested with the General Secretary (as an ex-officio trustee) reporting to the trustees. The Trust's work was divided into three areas – Finance and Administration; Promotion; and Research, Education and Information.

An advertising agency was also brought in for a year, free of charge, at the start of 1987 to boost NCCL's image and a new overall promotional strategy was devised. This was seen in some sections of the press as an attempt to reassert a waning influence on public opinion after a decade which witnessed, according to Sarah Spencer interviewed in the *Guardian* on 19 January 1989, the most sustained attack on civil liberties by any government since the war.

> This Government has done qualitative damage. It is a government neither receptive to civil libertarian arguments nor attached to protecting personal freedom. In the last Queen's Speech alone, eight out of the 16 Bills proposed had major civil liberties implications.

7 Liberty in the 1990s

On 24 January 1989 NCCL was relaunched as 'Liberty', at a press conference held at the Institute of Contemporary Arts in London, at which Sarah Spencer unveiled the group's strategy for the 1990s. The launch featured Harold Pinter (playwright), Rabbi Julia Neuberger, Norman Willis (General Secretary of the TUC), Robin Cook (Shadow Health Spokesperson) and Richard Shepherd (Conservative MP). The package included a new image, re-designed literature and a new logo. A book accompanied the event – *Decade of Decline: Civil Liberties in the Thatcher Years*, by Peter Thornton QC (Chair of NCCL, 1981/82). The re-launch received a mixed response in the press. *The Independent*, in particular, was scathing, referring to 'the designer logo, Liberty', and noting that the right-wing Freedom Association had been established, in part, to exploit NCCL's weakness during its internal divisions over the miners' strike.

The wisdom of changing NCCL's name was questioned by many at the time, including some staff members. The major difficulty with the old name was that it increasingly sounded like a government quango or a trade union co-ordinating body. To the man or woman in the street, NCCL did not appear to be an organisation they could join as members. Inevitably, acceptance and recognition of the new name was slow in coming and for several years both the old and new names tended to be used or, if the new name was used, the old one appeared in parentheses behind it. Further confusion arose because the name, Liberty, was the same as a leading London department store! Certainly, the change of name was a bold move and, overall, beneficial in eventually helping to project a more modern and dynamic image.

Meanwhile, campaigning and casework continued, though, in the area of women's rights, attitudes towards pornography revealed a further rift within the organisation. In 1988, Labour MP Clare Short, introduced a Bill to prohibit 'the display of pictures of naked or partially naked women in sexually provocative poses in newspapers'. This sparked a lengthy and lively debate in the letters column of *Civil Liberty* with supporters of the Bill arguing that such measures were necessary as a means of reducing violent attacks on women by men. Opponents – not all male – argued equally vociferously that attempts to introduce such controls amounted to censorship and an erosion of civil liberties and were counter to article seven of Liberty's own Charter of Civil Rights and Liberties.

The AGM in April 1988 remitted a motion which had severely criticised the Bill. However, the 1989 AGM passed a new policy on pornography, agree-

ing for the first time the need for legislation to control extreme forms de-
picting women as 'enjoying or deserving physical abuse'. This effectively represented the abandonment of Liberty's long-held policy against censorship
of any sort. By the 1990 AGM anti-censorship campaigners had re-grouped
and a motion was passed recognising the existence of sexism in society but
asserting that restraints on its expression in words and images did not reduce
the incidence of sexual discrimination in practice. The effect of these con-
flicting motions was, initially, an exodus of anti-censorship members and,
later, the departure of anti-pornography activists. The issue was eventually
settled in 1991 when a motion calling on Liberty to concentrate its efforts
on fighting sexual censorship in areas such as gay men's publications, comics,
material produced by women and sex education material was passed overwhelmingly.

Activities in other spheres remained as diverse as ever. March 1989 saw
the publication of *The Gibraltar Report: Inquest into the Deaths of Mairead
Farrell, Daniel McCann & Sean Savage, Gibraltar September 1988*, by Hilary
Kitchin (NCCL's legal observer at the inquest and a former Legal Officer),
published by Liberty and the International League for Human Rights. An interest in the personal privacy aspects of everyday life was maintained, as
illustrated by the 1987 report, *The Privacy Implications of the Poll Tax*. This
was to be a recurring theme, the August 1989 issue of *Civil Liberty* being
devoted to the topic and, in particular, to the requirements of poll tax reg-
istration forms.

After her successful efforts to redirect and restructure the NCCL as Liberty,
Sarah Spencer resigned as General Secretary in the summer of 1989. She was
succeeded that October by Andrew Puddephatt, formerly the leader of Hack-
ney Council, who immediately had to tackle another serious financial problem. The organisation's deficit was £90,000 in 1988 and £70,000 in 1989,
before breaking even in 1990. Staffing levels were slightly reduced from 16
to 14.5 at the end of 1990, although a new position of Press Officer was
created and taken up by an existing member of staff.

Recent cases and campaigns

During the early 1990s between one-third and one-half of the thousands of
cases dealt with annually by Liberty concerned criminal justice and, particularly, miscarriages of justice. Complaints against the police – which figured
so prominently in the 1960s and 1970s – represented a much smaller proportion of the whole. Funding of the advice and information service was

taken on by the Civil Liberties Trust, following a change in its trust deed. Most recently, in January 1994, Liberty launched a new *pro bono* panel of City solicitors firms who are prepared to take on test cases on civil liberties issues free of charge.

On the campaigning front, and on the advice of the new General Secretary, the EC agreed in 1990 that Liberty should concentrate its resources on a smaller number of priority areas, whilst maintaining a watchdog role in relation to other issues of interest. In effect, this was a belated recognition of the arrival on the scene of numerous single-issue pressure groups working in the field of civil liberties, making it essential that Liberty should have a much more responsive and flexible organisational approach to events and issues. Indeed, late 1990 also saw the loss of the last single-issue post in Liberty's establishment, namely the Women's Rights Officer.

This new strategy was immediately tested. The 'Civil Liberties in Time of War' campaign, introduced for the period of the Gulf War in early 1991, forced most of Liberty's other campaigning work to be abandoned. The success of this campaign helped to give Liberty its highest national profile for some time. About 180 Iraqi and other Middle Eastern nationals were detained, usually without charge, during the period of conflict on the grounds that they represented a state security risk. The detainees – some of whom were known opponents of the Iraqi régime – were also denied legal representation and threatened with deportation. Britain was the only allied nation to resort to such action. Liberty led a high profile campaign, in conjunction with other groups such as the Joint Council for the Welfare of Immigrants, and eventually the detainees were released in the early spring of 1991.

Regular use of European legal machinery has continued with varying degrees of success. Prior to the implementation of the single European market, the Civil Liberties Trust published *1992 and All That*, by Michael Spencer. Liberty also led the establishment of a British civil rights lobby to work at the European level and to operate in conjunction with other pressure groups, such as Charter 88, the JCWI, the Refugee Council and the SCCL. The UK Civil Rights Forum was launched in Brussels on 17 October 1990, discussion concentrating on the issues of policing in Europe and the social charter.

Northern Ireland has also remained firmly on the agenda. In conjunction with other groups, such as the SCCL, the Committee for the Administration of Justice and the Fédération Internationale de la Ligue des Droits de l'Homme, Liberty convened the Northern Ireland Human Rights Assembly in April 1992 at the Polytechnic of North London. Twelve Commissions examined breaches of human rights in relation to international covenants to which the UK is a signatory. The Assembly lasted three days, attracting several hundred people and 250 written submissions. On 28 June 1993 the NIHR Assembly report was published under the title *Broken Covenants* and launched in Belfast jointly with the Campaign for the Administration of Justice.

Support for a Bill of Rights and concern over breaches in human rights in Britain have also remained paramount. October 1991 saw the launch of *A People's Charter – Liberty's Bill of Rights*. Lobbying of (chiefly Labour) MPs and circulation of a briefing paper resulted in a commitment in the Labour Party's 1992 Election Manifesto to support a 'democratically enforced Bill of Rights'. The Labour Party also prepared a briefing paper for its prospective Parliamentary candidates in consultation with Liberty which was broadly in line with *A People's Charter*.

An additional use of international mechanisms characterises the Human Rights Convention campaign, launched, with a consortium of about 20 other campaigning bodies, in June 1993. This is a two-year campaign to highlight the British Government's human rights record in areas ranging from racism to discrimination against disabled people. A series of reports will be submitted to the United Nations Human Rights Committee in 1995. The first, produced jointly with MIND, and again reflecting a long-established interest, was *People with Mental Health Problems and Learning Disability*. Others published to date include *Criminal Justice and Civil and Political and Liberties,* in July 1993; *Racism: the Destruction of Civil and Political Liberties* (published jointly with Anti-Racist Alliance), in October 1993; *Democracy and Human Rights in the UK,* (published jointly with Charter 88), in February 1994; *Women's Rights, Human Rights* (published jointly with Change and Southall Black Sisters), in May 1994; and *Sexuality and the State* (published jointly with OutRage and Stonewall), in June 1994. The campaign was given impetus on 13 November 1993 by the highly successful 'Talking Liberties' conference in London, which comprised two plenary sessions and 17 workshops. About 500 representatives attended, and the topics covered included racism, women's rights, lesbian and gay rights, criminal justice, a Bill of Rights and the European Court.

A further campaign in support of the rights of gypsies and travellers was prompted by proposals by the Department of the Environment to repeal the Caravan Sites Act 1968. A 'Day of Action' was organised for 10 March 1993, when Liberty published *The Road to Nowhere,* and a mass lobby of the House of Commons drew between 500 and 600 gypsies and travellers. These events attracted considerable media interest – Andrew Puddephatt giving 21 television and radio interviews during the day.

However, probably the most important campaign in recent years has been around the issue of criminal justice. The establishment of the Royal Commission on Criminal Justice, chaired by Lord Runciman, was announced following the release in March 1991 of six long-term prisoners convicted of IRA bombings in Birmingham in November 1974, known as the 'Birmingham Six'. At the time it was thought that as many as 700 individuals who had been wrongly convicted were still serving long-term prison sentences[90] and it became clear that there was something deeply wrong with the British criminal justice system.

A campaign for changes in the system was launched at a press conference held at the House of Commons on 20 June 1991 and attended by several victims of miscarriages of justice, including three of the Birmingham Six. The following November Liberty submitted a detailed report to the Royal Commission entitled *Let Justice Be Done*. The Civil Liberties Trust also published *Unsafe and Unsatisfactory?*, which described 30 cases dealt with by the West Midlands Police Serious Crime Squad in which convictions had allegedly been obtained on the basis of uncorroborated confessional evidence.

In February 1992 the Miscarriage of Justice Network was launched in the columns of *Civil Liberty Agenda*. This campaign involved a petition and the establishment of a Civil Liberty Panel on Criminal Justice. Hearings of the Panel were attended by the Lord Chief Justice and members of the Royal Commission. A dossier of 111 cases was published in July 1992, drawing particular attention to the case of Winston Silcott, later to be cleared of the charge of murdering a policeman during the Broadwater Farm riot in Tottenham in 1985. One of Liberty's most ambitious projects for many years took place on 11 November 1992, named 'Justice Day' – a national day of action involving numerous events and personalities around the country. The proceedings began with a press conference and celebrity porridge breakfast in the Crypt of St Martin-in-the-Fields in London. *Justice on Trial: report of the Independent Civil Liberty Panel on Criminal Justice*, edited by Peter Thornton QC, Ann Mallalieu QC and Anthony Scrivener QC, was published on the same day and in the afternoon Liberty presented its verbal evidence to the Royal Commission.

On 10-12 July 1993 Liberty and other groups, including Justice, Amnesty International, Charter 88 and the Bar Council, organised a major rally and lobby of Parliament to coincide with the publication of the Runciman Report. This was swiftly followed by the publication of the second of Liberty's Human Rights Convention reports (on criminal justice), meetings with friends and relatives of victims of miscarriages of justice, and the presentation by Andrew

Puddephatt of a petition of 15,000 signatures to the Home Office. The subsequent publication of the Criminal Justice and Public Order Bill in December 1993 prompted Liberty and other groups to mount a challenge to most of its proposals – initially concentrating on the threat to end the right of silence of accused persons.

The positive note on which Liberty entered its seventh decade of existence was perhaps best shown by the introduction of its annual Human Rights Award, named in memory of its former General Secretary, Martin Ennals. This award was intended to honour the person or group considered to have made the most significant contribution to civil liberties during the preceding year. On Human Rights Day 1991 (10 December) it was presented by Lord Ennals (brother of Martin Ennals) to Breda Power, daughter of one of the Birmingham Six and a leader of the Birmingham Six Campaign. In 1992 the Award was given to the Southall Black Sisters for their work in support of Asian women and in 1993 to the Burnsall Strikers for their efforts to gain union recognition and equal pay.

8 Conclusion

It is difficult to believe that this remarkable story is the result of one man's initiative back in January 1934 when the Council for Civil Liberties was formed. Ronald Kidd could hardly have guessed that 60 years later the organisation that he founded would still be widely regarded as one of Britain's most effective and successful pressure groups.

Of course, every organisation has its ups and downs. The strengths and weaknesses of Liberty and its forerunner have been amply demonstrated during its first 60 years of existence. It has never achieved a truly mass membership and, even after the change of name, has not generally been considered a membership organisation. At the time of writing, Liberty has 5,250 individual members, plus a further 425 affiliated organisations. For long periods, its image – whatever the reality – has been that of a predominantly white, middle-class and university-educated group of well meaning, if sometimes misguided, campaigners. Its activities in support of groups and individuals who might generally be termed 'unpopular' have perhaps mitigated against it securing a greater level of popularity.

Battles of and for liberty inevitably bring conflict with authority, whether ministers, politicians or civil servants, or even the establishment press. This was the basis of the frequent charges that the NCCL was a front for the Communist Party. Those wishing to discover hard evidence of manipulation by, or consultation with, the CPGB over NCCL policy will not find it in the surviving NCCL archives nor, I suspect, anywhere else – apart, of course, from the deeply suspicious and undoubtedly biased reports of members of MI5 and Special Branch, held elsewhere.

The reality of the situation is much more complex. As Barry Cox pointed out in April 1974

> ...it is one of the great assets of the NCCL that it has managed to hang together an amazing coalition which in any other area just couldn't coexist. But it has proved possible for 40 years to keep Tories – admittedly liberal Tories – and Communists, and I[nternational] S[ocialists] and Trotskyists in the same camp.[91]

It is also true to say that, in the public mind, support for the liberties of those espousing a particular cause automatically means support for the cause itself, a condition frequently exploited by some politicians and members of the press.

On the positive side – and overwhelmingly so – the organisation quickly grew into, and remains, an effective agency of public and individual protest with a supporting machinery that can harness the use of observation, publicity, the analysis of legislation, the lobbying of Parliament, the support of legal cases and, when necessary, the use of mass protest to achieve its aims.

Compared with the early 1930s, we now have a much more mature and questioning, some might say cynical society. There are still vestiges of the deference and class consciousness which dominated everyday life at that time. But at least pressure groups such as Liberty now exist to help to protect those whose rights are breached and to act as watchdogs in anticipation of such infringements of liberties.

So what of the future? CH Rolph, reviewing the NCCL *Annual Report* for *New Law Journal* on 11 April 1974, wondered if the Council would still exist in 2074. His conclusion is still appropriate:

> Yes, because it has become socially, politically and deservedly important.
> If it didn't exist it would be necessary to invent it without delay. If it died,
> a successor would have to be organised at once.

Notes

1. Its journal, *Link: a journal for the servants of man* (edited by Annie Besant and WT Stead), ran from February to December, 1888

2. See Robbins, Keith, *The Abolition of War: the 'peace movement' in Britain 1914-1919* (Cardiff, University of Wales Press, 1976)

3. Scaffardi, Sylvia, *Fire Under the Carpet: working for civil liberties in the thirties* (London, Lawrence & Wishart, 1986), p29

4. Cockburn, Claud, 'Civil liberties', 23 Feb 1955, p263 *Punch*

5. The Metropolitan Police file held in the Public Record Office (reference MEPO 3/553) includes papers relating to this affair, with copies of the articles and correspondence

6. *Ibid.*

7. Letter from Ronald Kidd to Douglas Goldring, 12 February 1934, DCL (recent addition)

8. Undated agenda paper for meeting of 22 Feb 1934 in the NCCL archive, Brynmor Jones Library, University of Hull, at reference DCL/74/1

9. NCCL, *Annual Report* 1934/35, p7

10. Scaffardi, *op. cit.*, p22

11. DCL/74/1

12. *Annual Report* 1934/35, p31

13. Scaffardi, *op. cit.*, p20

14. Cockburn, *op. cit.*

15. Martin, Kingsley, *Editor: a second volume of autobiography, 1931-45* (London, Hutchinson, 1968), p154

16. PRO MEPO 3/553

17. Cockburn, *op. cit.*

18. Scaffardi, *op. cit.*, p85

19. Council for Civil Liberties, 'The Incitement to Disaffection Bill', c. April 1934, in DCL/2/1, p1

20. Copies of the correspondence in June and July 1934 are to be found in DCL/2/1

21. DCL/74/1

22. Reported in *Civil Liberty*, V.42 No.1, Feb 1976, p3

23. *The Special Powers Acts of Northern Ireland: report of a Commission of Inquiry* ... (London, NCCL, 1936); NCCL papers are held at DCL/72

24. DCL/18/2

25. *Duncan v. Jones* (1936) 1 King's Bench 218; the case was reported in the NCCL's *News Sheet* No.2 (Oct 1935), p5, no.18/19 (Aug.1936), pp5-6, and is discussed in Kidd, Ronald, *British Liberty in Danger*, (London, Lawrence & Wishart, 1940) pp22-24 and Hewitt, Patricia, *The Abuse of Power* ... (Oxford, Martin Robertson, 1982) pp123-124

26. DCL/40/1

27. DCL/38/4

28. DCL/7/2-3

29. *Ibid.*

30. The *News Sheet* is extremely rare, but there is a set in the archive at DCL/48/1

31. The paper dates from c. October 1935, DCL/9/2

32. Files at DCL/9/4 and 74/8; report entitled *The Thurloe Square Baton Charge: report of a Commission of Inquiry* (London, NCCL, 1936)

33. PRO MEPO 2/3089, file on Thurloe Square demonstration

34. DCL/27/1-3; report entitled *The Harworth Colliery Strike: a report to the Executive Committee of the National Council for Civil Liberties* (London, NCCL, 1937)

35. Extracts are reproduced in *The Strange Case of Major Vernon* (London, NCCL, 1937)

36. DCL/67/11

37. Scaffardi, *op. cit.*, p108

38. DCL/76/4

39. DCL/62/5

40. DCL/259/2

41. DCL/312/1

42. PRO MEPO 3/553

43. Reported in *Civil Liberty* V.6 No.3, June 1990, p1

44. DCL/32/5

45. All these references relating to the charge of Communist bias are in file DCL/32/8; Laski, Harold, *Freedom of the Press in Wartime* (London, NCCL, 1941)

46. Scaffardi, *op. cit.* p185

47. Kidd, Ronald, *The Fight for a Free Press* (London, NCCL, 1942)

48. A press cuttings book of obituaries survives at DCL/305/4

49. DCL/41/4

50. *Parliamentary Debates* 1 Dec 1943, V.395 No.4, p474

51. DCL/41/4(a)

52. DCL/32/9

53. *Ibid*, and 41/4(a)

54. DCL/32/10 and 266 (minute book)

55. DCL/77/3 and 266

56. Described in *The Story of the Cairo Forces' Parliament* (London, NCCL, 1945) and Spector, RJ, *Freedom for the Forces* (London, NCCL, 1947)

57. DCL/6/3

58. DCL/32/13

59. *Ibid.*

60. *Ibid.*

61. DCL/32/11

62. *Civil Liberty* V.7.No.11, Sept 1947, p3

63. Royal Commission on the Law Relating to Mental Illness and Mental Deficiency. *Minutes of Evidence*, days 22 and 27 (London: HMSO, 1955)

64. DCL/34/7

65. *Civil Liberty* V.12 No.5, Spring 1956

66. Transcript of interview with Barry Cox, 1974 (DCL)

67. *Civil Liberty* V.5 No.3, June 1989

68. Transcript of interview with John Tùchfeld, 1974 (DCL)

69. DCL/114/8

70. Hurwitt, Malcolm 'The Cobden Trust', in Lilly, M, *The National Council for Civil Liberties: the first fifty years* (London, Macmillan, 1984) p156

71. Cobden Trust *Annual Report,* 1979

72. *Civil Liberty* V.4 No.4 (Oct 1943), p3

73. Reported in *Civil Liberty* V.10 No.2 Feb/Mar 1950

74. Transcript of interview with Tony Smythe, 1974 (DCL)

75. DCL/500/13

76. See Saville, John, 'The Council for Academic Freedom and Democracy', in Lilly, *op. cit.,* pp152-154

77. NCCL produced the pamphlet *Reluctant Servicemen* (London, Housmans & NCCL, 1967)

78. The statements are at DCL/243-250; there are also transcripts of the official Widgery Tribunal held 14 Feb - 3 Mar 1972 at DCL/251-252, with a copy of the Widgery *Report* and *Justice Denied* in DCL/252.

79. Reported in *Civil Liberty* V.41 No.2 (April 1975) p2

80. 'Report on allocation of responsibilities within the office' (DCL)

81. *Individual Privacy: evidence to the Data Protection Committee* (London, NCCL, 1977)

82. Dummett, Michael, et al., *Southall: 23 April 1979* (London, NCCL, 1980)

83. Thornton, Peter, *Decade of Decline: Civil Liberties in the Thatcher Years* (London, NCCL, 1989), p91

84. Reported in NCCL *Annual Report* 1981, p5

85. *Rights,* V.7 No.2 (Summer 1983), p1

86. Gostin, Larry, *A Human Condition: the Mental Health Act from 1959 to 1975* (London, MIND, 1976)

87. Letter from John Bennett in *Civil Liberty* V.1 No.2 (March 1985)

88. Eventually published as: McCabe, S and Wallington, P, eds, *The Police, Public Order and Civil Liberties* (London, Routledge, 1988)

89. The disputes are covered in *Civil Liberty* V.1 No.4 (June 1985) and Gostin, Larry, ed., *Civil Liberties in Conflict* (London, Routledge, 1988), pp14-20 and 117-120

90. Liberty *Annual Record*

91. Transcript of Barry Cox interview (DCL)

Appendix 1: Chronology

1934

January: Ronald Kidd makes initial contacts with prominent individuals such as Kingsley Martin and Henry Nevinson and establishes embryonic Council for Civil Liberties. The CCL and *Free Speech & Assembly Bulletin* commence operations from Kidd's home at 3 Dansey Place, off Shaftesbury Avenue.

February 22: First formal meeting of the Council held at St Martin-in-the Fields, Trafalgar Square. Executive Committee elected and Kidd confirmed as Secretary.

February 24: Letter announcing the formation of the Council appears in the *Manchester Guardian.*

February 25: CCL observers – including HG Wells, Harold Laski and Vera Brittain – oversee the arrival of hunger marchers in Hyde Park. EM Forster agrees to become President.

May: CCL organises national campaign against the Sedition Bill, comprising mass meetings, conferences and deputations.

June: Begin to monitor fascist meetings and anti-Jewish activity, following meeting held by Sir Oswald Mosley's BUF at Olympia on 7 June.

July 10-11: Independent Commission chaired by Aylmer Digby KC investigates Olympia meeting.

July 30: Mrs Kath Duncan arrested for obstruction. First major individual case taken up by NCCL – eventually lost on appeal in 1936.

November 6: Mock Sedition trial held at Friends Meeting House, Euston Road, featuring David Low, Miles Malleson and others.

Other campaigns: Non-flam films; support for delegation from the Gold Coast (later Ghana).

Publications
The Incitement to Disaffection Act – How it Now Stands
Non-Flam Films

1935

January: Commission of Inquiry into the operation of the Special Powers Act in Northern Ireland commences, chaired by Aylmer Digby KC, begins work.

April: Move office to 99a Charing Cross Road, WC2.

June: Outbreaks of sectarian rioting in Belfast witnessed by Kidd.

August: New publication for members entitled *News Sheet.*

1936

January: Henry Nevinson succeeds Forster as President.

March 22: Police baton-charge anti-fascist demonstrators in Thurloe Square.

July: NCCL conduct own inquiry into Thurloe Square incidents under chairmanship of Professor Norman Bentwich.

September: Strike begins at Harworth Colliery in Nottinghamshire.

Other campaigns: Public Order Bill.

Publications
The Special Powers Acts of Northern Ireland: report of a Commission of Inquiry

1937

January: Move office to Morley House, 320 Regent Street. Kidd visits Harworth Colliery to investigate complaints against the police.

April 23-24: Disturbances at Harworth result in arrest of strike leaders.

May-June: NCCL organises Defence of Harworth Colliery strikers, but fails to prevent heavy sentences.

July 9: Launch petition with London Trades Council and the Mineworkers' Federation of Great Britain in support of the Harworth men.

July 14: First use under Public Order Act of 1936 covering use of 'insulting words and behaviour' at Stepney Green.

September 8: Kidd delivers petition containing 250,880 signatures to the Home Office in support of the Harworth men. First issue of new quarterly journal entitled *Civil Liberty,* incorporating *News sheet* and *Free speech & assembly bulletin.*

October 23: Major Wilfred Vernon convicted under the Official Secrets Act.

November: Vernon dismissed from the Civil Service. Kidd knocked down by a car whilst on his way to address a meeting in Hampstead.

Publications
The Harworth Colliery Strike, by Ronald Kidd

1938

March: Conference on Conditions in Trinidad (following disturbances in June 1937).

November: Conference on Freedom of the Press and the Official Secrets Act.

December: Kidd suffers health breakdown.

Other campaign: Supports right of asylum to Austrian and other refugees wishing to escape Nazi control.

Publications
The Strange Case of Major Vernon
Freedom of the Press and the Official Secrets Act
The Use of the Police for Political Purposes

1939

February 18: Conference on the Civil Rights of Black-Coated Workers – attracts 433 delegates.

August: Emergency Powers Act passed.

October: Several civil defence colour bar cases highlighted by NCCL.

November: Preliminary conference on Civil Liberty in Wartime, attended by 778 people.

1940

January: Move offices to 37 Great James Street, Bedford Row, WC1.

March: Monthly news letter (for branches) launched.

June 1: Delegate Conference on 'Civil Liberty in the Armed Forces'.

July 21: Emergency conference on wartime emergency – attracts 1300 people.

August 24: Conference on Civil Liberty and the Defeat of Fascism – attracts over 1500 delegates representing nearly two million people at Central Hall, Westminster.

By the end of the year the membership total reaches about 3000, plus over 700 affiliated organisations.

Publication
British Liberty in Danger, by Ronald Kidd

1941

January: First issue of *Quarterly Case Book* ('Liberty Campaign issue'). Kidd's health deteriorates – Nancy Bell deputises for several months.

People's Convention followed by BBC banning of artists involved.

February: NCCL strongly opposes supression of the *Daily Worker.* Conference on Civil Liberty in the Colonial Empire held at Conway Hall – attracts some 235 delegates.

March 17: Organises protest meeting in the Conway Hall against BBC ban.

March 20: Winston Churchill effectively ends the BBC ban.

May 13: Harold Laski resigns from the Executive Committee, claiming Communist influence. Public allegations of Communist infiltration persist for the rest of the year.

June 7: Conference with the NUJ on the Freedom of the Press.

August: Sylvia Crowther-Smith resigns as Assistant Secretary.

September: Move office to 11a Kings Road, Sloane Square, SW7. Financial crisis – *Civil Liberty* appears as a two-sheet cyclo-styled emergency edition.

November 9: Henry Nevinson dies. Kidd 'promoted' to new post of Director. Elizabeth Acland Allen takes over as General Secretary.

Publications
Civil Liberties Offended
The Internment and Treatment of Aliens
Freedom of the Press in Wartime, by Harold Laski

1942

March: AGM adopts new constitution, introducing annual elections by postal ballot for the EC. Forster returns as President, for one year only.

April 11: Meeting on press freedom in Central Hall, Westminster – 3000 attend.

May 12: Death of Ronald Kidd, aged 53. Tributes include BBC broadcast by Kingsley Martin.

Publications
The Fight for a Free Press, by Ronald Kidd
Civil Liberty and the Industrial Worker, by Angela Tuckett

1943

March 17: Conference, It Shall Not Happen Here, – starts nationwide campaign against anti-semitism and fascism and attracts 443 delegates. Associated pamphlet by Elizabeth Allen sells 25,000 copies by the end of the war.

November: Release from internment of Sir Oswald Mosley condemned officially by NCCL but many members oppose imprisonment without trial. Conference on Juvenile Courts attracts 606 delegates to Friends' Meeting House.

Other campaign: Colour Bar (case of Leary Constantine).

Publications
It Shall Not Happen Here: Anti-Semitism, Fascists and Civil Liberty, by Elizabeth
A Allen

1944

June: Peace Pledge Union resigns its membership over the George Elphick
case and NCCL's failure to support 'justified' law-breakers.

November: NCCL fails to support Tyneside apprentices (and Trotskyists) imprisoned under the 1927 Trade Disputes Act.

Other campaign: Opposes anti-Semitism in the Polish Armed Forces.

Publications
Absentees for Freedom, by Tom Driberg
Civil Liberties Defended

1945

October 30: Conference on civil liberty in the colonies.

Publications
Local Government and Civil Liberty: the Citizen's Rights and Duties Explained,
by Elizabeth A Allen
Civil Liberty and the Colonies
The Story of the Cairo Forces' Parliament.
Black Chattels, by Geoffrey Parsons

1946

May: Nancy Bell resigns after along illness.

November 10: Meeting in support of democratic rights for the armed forces
held at Palace Theatre, Cambridge Circus – speakers include Lt James Callaghan.

1947

March: Death of Nancy Bell.

June 13-16: NCCL organises International Conference on Human Rights –
69 delegates attend, representing 15 countries and four British Colonies.

August: Death of WH Thompson.

November 22/23: National Conference on Human Rights at St Pancras Town
Hall – attracts 300 delegates to St Pancras Town Hall.

Other campaign: NCCL takes up first major mental health case – 'Jane'.

Publications
Freedom for the Forces, by RJ Spector

1948

March 20: Only 147 attend AGM – main issue is political discrimination in the civil service.

April 30: Resignation of EM Forster following revived charge of Communist influence.

Renewed financial crisis, with urgent appeal for funds in *Civil Liberty,* which began to carry advertisements for the first time.

Publications
The Purge (NCCL Civil Service Branch)

1949

January 22: Conference on Freedom of Speech at Beaver Hall – 240 delegates attend.

July: John McGrath wins appeal after being wrongfully imprisoned for receiving stolen goods, with campaign organised by NCCL and John McGrath Appeal Committee.

NCCL arranges defence of 14 blacks charged with affray, following racial discrimination incidents at Carrington House in Deptford – further investigations and a Conference at Goldsmiths College on 6 December.

November: Office moves to 46 Westbourne Grove, Bayswater, W2.

1950

June 10: Conference on Mental Deficiency – attracts more than 200 delegates. Topic dominates NCCL's activities for most of the 1950s.

Publications
Civil Servants and Politics

1951

April: First reluctant servicemen cases highlighted by mass break out of boy soldiers from the RASC at Aldershot.

August: Second conference on mental deficiency laws held.

Publications
50,000 Outside the Law

1952

June: Campaign against repressive racist legislation in South Africa begins with protest meeting in London.

July: Conference on South Africa – attended by 130 delegates.

Summer: Financial crisis – urgent appeal for funds to prevent office having to close for the summer.

September 30: South Africa Protest Day – thousands of letters of protest delivered to South Africa House.

1953

Continued campaign against the colour bar in hotels, public houses, etc.

Appointment of Royal Commission on Mental Health announced.

1954

February: 21st birthday celebrations held at Charing Cross Hotel.

NCCL's lengthy memorandum of evidence submitted to the Royal Commission on Mental Health.

Publications
The Case of Dr Cort
Handbook of Citizen's Rights

1955

March: NCCL's three witnesses give oral evidence to the Royal Commission for a whole day, with a follow-up in June.

Publications
By What Authority?

1956

January: Following NCCL campaign, Emery, Powers and Thompson receive royal pardon after being wrongfully convicted of attacking a policeman.

February: NCCL obtains a successful writ of *habeas corpus* on behalf of Kathleen Rutty. A further 590 similar cases revealed within months.

June 30: Conference on Mental Deficiency Laws – over 200 delegates.

Publications
It isn't Colour Bar but...

1957

May: Royal Commission on Mental Health reports, vindicating NCCL's lengthy campaign.

October 26: Further Conference on Mental Deficiency – over 150 delegates.

November: Allen appears on television to oppose state telephone tapping. Move into temporary offices on Edgware Road.

1958

May: Again move office, this time to 293 New Kings Road, SW6.

Persistent ill-health leads Allen to become Hon. Secretary at her own request.

1959

February 24: Death of Frank Haskell, architect of the Mental Health Campaign.

November: Colour Bar Conference held at Friends' Meeting House – attended by 210 delegates.

Mental Health Act introduces Mental Health Review Tribunals, at which NCCL volunteers regularly represent patients.

Highways Act makes it an offence to camp on the highway, including verges.

Publications
Immigration – Discrimination or Integration

1960

February: Conference on Anti-Semitism and Racial Incitement at Friends' House – 121 delegates.

November: NCCL submits detailed written and oral evidence to the Royal Commission on Police, calling above all for the introduction of procedures to ensure an effective system of complaint and redress.

DN Pritt retires from the Executive Committee after nearly 26 years.

Martin Ennals succeeds Elizabeth Allen as General Secretary.

Freedom of speech and assembly becomes a major civil liberties issue following activities of CND and the Committee of 100.

Individual membership below 2000, but two million represented through affiliated bodies. Three full-time members of staff.

Civil Liberty resumes regular production as a two-page cyclo-styled newsletter, having doubled as *Annual Report* for many years.

Publications
Anti-Semitism and Colour Bar – a Warning
Arrest: a Guide to the Citizen's Rights

1961

Publication of pamphlet *Public Order and the Police* calls for public enquiry into police tactics against Committee of 100.

1962

Commonwealth Immigrants Act greatly curtails black immigration.

Support for groups banned from holding rallies or meetings in Trafalgar Square and for six organisers of the Committee of 100 arrested whilst attempting to organise a sit-down protest at a US air base.

Publications
Security and the Individual

1963

May: Cobden Trust founded as charity and research arm.

October: NCCL submits memorandum to Departmental Committee on Jury Service, pressing for greater representation, particularly for women and poor people.

Challenor 'half-brick' cases first come to light.

Parliamentary Civil Liberties Group founded.

Move offices to 4 Camden High Street.

Publications
Are You a Security Risk?
Civil Liberty and the Police
Is it Justice?

1964

Publication of new edition of *Handbook of Citizens' Rights* – press report suggestions that under certain circumstances members of the public are entitled to run away from the police.

1965

March: Conference on Northern Ireland – investigates allegations of discrimination against Catholics.

Close monitoring of anti-Vietnam War demonstrations held in and around the US Embassy in Grosvenor Square.

Group of gypsies in Orpington summonsed for being on the public highway having been put there by the local authority.

Publications
The Challenor Case, by Mary Grigg.
Prejudice or Principle – the Government's Policy on Race
Local Government and Civil Liberty
Women

1966

Martin Ennals leaves – succeeded as General Secretary by Tony Smythe.

Malcolm B Purdie is made President after being Chair of the Executive Committee for 15 years.

May: Reluctant servicemen again major issue – case of Leading Engineer John Mayhew brings press and television campaign and leads to exposure of many other cases and appointment of the Donaldson Committee.

Publications
The James Report

1967

Promotions Officer appointed.

Northern Ireland Civil Rights Association set up.

Publications
Drugs and Civil Liberties
The Rights of Children and Young Persons, by Nan Berger (Cobden Trust)
Reluctant Servicemen

1968

UN Human Rights Year.

Commonwealth Immigrants Act – places further controls on black immigration.

June: Emergency 'Speak out on race' meeting at Friends' Meeting House following Enoch Powell's 'rivers of blood' speech.

December: Tony Smythe leads a delegation to present a petition and 'Declaration on Race' to the Prime Minister.

Major campaign on privacy.

Caravan Sites Act steered through Parliament by Eric Lubbock, chair of the PCLG.

Publications
Arrest
Privacy Under attack
On the Road, by Grattan Puxon

1969

January: Scottish Council for Civil Liberties established.
August: Introduction of British Army in place of police in Belfast.
November: Move offices to 152 Camden High Street.

Publications
The Police and the Citizen

1970

February: Executive Committee agrees to deposit historical archive in Brynmor Jones Library after prolonged negotiations with Philip Larkin.
October: Council for Academic Freedom and Democracy launched as an offshoot of NCCL.
Conference organised with the National Computing Centre entitled 'The Data Bank Society'. NCCL gives evidence to the Younger Committee on Privacy.

Publications
Civil Liberties and Service Recruitment

1971

August: Introduction of internment in Northern Ireland.
Immigration Act again restricts black immigration.

Publications
Bail or Custody, by Michael King and Christine Jackson (Cobden Trust)

1972

January 30: 'Bloody Sunday' – 13 killed in Londonderry. NCCL obtains evidence from over 600 witnesses, which is supplied to Sam Dash for his report entitled *Justice denied*, in response to the official Widgery Tribunal held in February and March 1972.
NCCL's 1936 Northern Ireland report reprinted.

December 10: Ramsey Clark, US Attorney-General under President Johnson, delivers first Human Rights Day Lecture organised by the Cobden Trust.

Tony Smythe resigns on his appointment as Director of MIND (the National Association for Mental health).

Staff numbers reach 15, and individual membership 5400.

Publications

Civil Liberty: the NCCL guide, edited by Anna Coote and Lawrence Grant, published by Penguin Books.

Against Censorship

Civil Liberties and the Judges Rules, by Peter Thornton QC

The Rights of Suspects

Rights of Children: Report of the First National Conference on Children's Rights, edited by Mark Vaughan

1973

January: Martin Loney becomes General Secretary.

April: Move offices to 186 Kings Cross Road, WC1X 9DE

Establishment of Women's Rights Sub-Committee

September: Appointment of Patricia Hewitt as first Women's Rights Officer.

Membership suddenly falls. Reduction in external grants announced by Rowntree Social Service Trust.

Publications

Women's Rights, by Patricia Hewitt

Against Birching: Judicial Corporal Punishment in the Isle of Man, by Angela Kneale

Justice in Northern Ireland, by Tom Hadden and Paddy Hillyard (Cobden Trust)

1974

February: Conference on Women, Trade Unions and Work, and associated pamphlet entitiled *Danger: Women at Work*. Foreign husbands campaign begins.

April: Police informer, Kenneth Lennon, found dead in a ditch in Surrey two days after giving a lengthy statement about his underground activities to NCCL's Legal Officer.

June: Martin Loney dismissed as General Secretary – succeeded by Patricia Hewitt (initially on a temporary basis).

September: Special General Meeting confirms dismissal of Loney.

December: Hewitt confirmed as General Secretary. Financial crisis results in loss of five posts.

Direct rule introduced in Northern Ireland.

Gay Rights Committee formed, followed by appointment of Gay Rights Organiser and launch of Gay Rights Campaign.

Publications
Danger! Women at Work, edited by Patricia Hewitt
Whose Conspiracy?, by Geoffrey Robertson
Protection of Minors: a Case Against Corporal Punishment
Conspiracy and Civil Liberties, by Robert Hazell (Cobden Trust)

1975

January: Scottish Council for Civil Liberties becomes fully independent.

Purchase of five million personal credit files from Konfax Limited for one penny.

December: Fourteen members of the British Withdrawal from Northern Ireland Movement acquitted on incitement to disaffection charges, some represented by NCCL.

Case of Veronica Pickles establishes right of a lesbian midwife to become a health visitor.

Publications
The Children's Ombudsman
Homosexuality and the Teaching Profession
Rights for Woman, by Patricia Hewitt
Equal Pay and How to Get it, by Ruth Lister and Marion Lowe
Battered Women – How to Use the Law, by Tess Gill and Anna Coote (Cobden Trust)

1976

Civil Liberty becomes *Rights*

Publications
Maternity Rights for Working Women, by Jean Coussins
The Unequal Breadwinner: a New Perspective on Women and Social Security, by Ruth Lister and Leo Wilson
The Prevention of Terrorism Acts 1974 and 1976, by Catherine Scorer
Civil Liberties and a Bill of Rights, by Peter Wallington and Jeremy McBride (Cobden Trust)
Incitement to Disaffection, by T Young and M Kettle (Cobden Trust)
Squatting, Trespass and Civil Liberties

1977

December: membership at 4,765. Major appeals to stave off threatened bankruptcy.

Evidence to the Lindop Data protection Committee (reported 1978). Launch 'Right to Know' Campaign.

Publications
Homosexuality and the Social Services, by Dave Ferris
Privacy: the Information-Gatherers, by Patricia Hewitt
The Protection of Human Rights in the United Kingdom, by Sir Leslie Scarman (Cobden Trust)

1978

Number of staff falls to nine full-time and four part-time.

Publications
Sex Discrimination in Schools, by Harriet Harman
A Practical Guide to the Race Relations Act, by Patricia Hewitt, Ann Sedley and John Wright
Your Rights at Work: a Practical Guide, by Patricia Hewitt

1979

April 23: Death of Blair Peach during anti-National Front demonstration at Southall. NCCL sets up independent inquiry under Professor Michael Dummett in July (reported April 1980). Public inquiry refused.

Publications
Rights, Responsibilities and the Law, edited by Judith Edmunds (Cobden Trust)
Justice Deserted: the Subversion of the Jury, by Harriet Harman and JAG Griffith
Income Tax and Sex Discrimnation, by Patricia Hewitt
The Politics of Secrecy, by Michael James
First Rights: a Guide to Legal Rights for Young People, by Maggie Rae, Patricia Hewitt and B Hugill

1980

First full-time Gay Rights Officer appointed.

Harriet Harman (Legal Officer) prosecuted for Contempt of Court for leaking evidence to the press which had already been read out in open court. Harman eventually vindicated by the European Commission.

Publications
Southall, 23 April 1979: the Report of the Unofficial Committee of Enquiry, Chair: Michael Dummett
Drifting Into a Law and Order Society, by Stuart Hall (Cobden Trust)
In Whose Best Interests?: the Unjust Treatment of Children in Courts and Institutions, by Laurie Taylor, Ron Lacey and Denis Bracken (Cobden Trust)

1981

November: Offices move to permanent premises at 21 Tabard Street.

British Nationality Act further restricts black immigration.

'Sus' law repealed.

Increasing use of the European Convention on Human Rights – publication of *An Effective Remedy? – a Review of the Procedure of the ECHR*, followed in November by a seminar on the topic at the Royal Commonwealth Society in London.

Publications
Gay Workers: Trade Unions and the Law, Chris Beer and others
An Effective Remedy? – a Review of the Procedure of the ECHR
The Price of Justice, by Howard Levenson (Cobden Trust)

1982

May: Series of test cases lodged with the European Commission as part of continuing Foreign Husbands Campaign organised jointly with the JCWI.

August: NCCL supports application to the European Commission by Kathleen Stewart following the death of her 13 year-old son, hit by a plastic bullet in Belfast in October 1976.

Financial crisis reflected in reduced size of *Rights*.

Publications
Whose File is it Anyway?, by Ruth Cohen
A Fair Cop: Reforming the Police Complaints Procedure, by Patricia Hewitt
Sexual Harassment at Work, by Ann Sedley and Melissa Benn
Immigration Law and Practice, by Lawrence Grant and Ian Martin (Cobden Trust)

1983

June: Patricia Hewitt leaves to stand for Parliament – Sarah Spencer made acting General Secretary.

GLC funds Gay Community Policing Project.

Publications
Judging Women: a Study of Attitudes that Rule our Legal Profession, by Patty Pattullo
The Use and Abuse of Emergency Legislation in Northern Ireland, by Dermot Walsh (Cobden Trust)

1984

January: Dr Larry Gostin becomes General Secretary.

February: Golden Jubilee celebrations and Liberty Campaign featuring new Charter of Civil Rights and Freedoms boosts membership by over 1000, and sees the re-launch of the All-Party Civil Liberties Group.

April: Customs & Excise Officers confiscate stock of Gay's the Word Bookshop. With NCCL support and representation, all charges eventually dropped and the books returned in June 1986.

AGM establishes independent Inquiry into the policing of the Miners' Strike under the Chairmanship of Professor Peter Wallington. Interim Report published later in the year.

Other matters of controversy include: ban on trade union membership at GCHQ Cheltenham and advice policy in relation to known members of the National Front.

Publications
Supergrasses: the Use of Accomplice Evidence in Northern Ireland, by Tony Gifford (Cobden Trust)
Troops in Strikes: Military Intervention in Industrial Disputes, by Steve Peak (Cobden Trust)
Civil Liberties and the Miners' Dispute: first report of the Independent Inquiry
Civil Rights for Civil Servants

1985

February: *Rights* re-named *Civil Liberty*.

Acquittal of Clive Ponting under Official Secrets Act – his Defence Fund had been launched by NCCL and others.

April: Controversial AGM supports EC's view that the Wallington Inquiry had exceeded its brief. Members of the Inquiry team decide to work independently of NCCL.

May: Resignation of Larry Gostin – claiming that NCCL had been taken over by the left. Sarah Spencer made acting General Secretary (made permanent in July).

October: Broadwater Farm riots and death of PC Keith Blakelock – NCCL advises the Defence Campaign.

Attempts by National Front to infiltrate NCCL results in rejection of membership applications by EC.

Publications

Data Protection: Putting the Record Straight, by R Cornwell and Marie Staunton

Black Magistrates: a Study of Selection and Appointment, by Michael King and Colin May (Cobden Trust)

Called to Account: the Case for Police Accountability in England and Wales, by Sarah Spencer

We Protest: the Public Order Debate, by Peter Thornton QC

Policing the Miners' Strike, edited by Bob Fine and Robert Millar (Cobden Trust)

1986

March: Demise of Greater London Council causes considerable financial crisis and appeal for funds. Three GLC-funded (temporary) posts lost.

September: Actress Glenda Jackson visits Tabard Street, joins NCCL, and launches new membership drive. Membership reaches 8000.

Provide observers during the Wapping News International dispute. Also support 'New Age' travellers following incidents at Stonehenge and elsewhere.

Publications

Abolishing the Diplock Courts, by Steven C Greer and A White (Cobden Trust)

No Way in Wapping: the Effects of the Policing of the News International Dispute on Wapping Residents

Stonehenge: a Report into the Civil Liberties Implications of the Events Relating to the Convoys of Summer 1985 and 1986

Positive Action: Changing the Workplace for Women, by Paddy Stamp and Sadie Roberts

Strip Searching: an Inquiry into the Strip Searching of Women Remand Prisoners at Armagh Prison between 1982 and 1985

1987

June: Organises public readings of the banned *Spycatcher*, by Peter Wright.

Supports journalist Duncan Campbell following banning of his BBC film on the Zircon spy satellite.

Launch Bill of Rights campaign.

Oppose new Public Order Act.

Issue General Election leaflet detailing Conservative civil rights record.

Management consultants bought in to re-structure staffing organisation. Advertising agency brought in to boost image.

Cobden Trust re-named Civil Liberties Trust.

Publications
The Conservative Government's Record on the Protection and Extension of Civil Liberties
The Privacy Implications of the Poll Tax
The Civil Liberties of the Zircon Affair, by Peter Thornton QC

1988

July: Management re-structuring takes place

Killing in Gibraltar of three suspected IRA members.

Challenged the surveillance by MI5 of Patricia Hewitt and Harriet Harman in European Court.

Affiliated to the Federation Internationale des Droits de l'Homme as part of new strategy involving greater use of the international human rights machinery.

Jointly campaigned with other organisations against Clause 28 of the Local Government Bill which prohibited the 'promotion of homosexuality' by local authorities.

Strong support for anti-pornography campaign.

Publications
Section 28: a Practical Guide to the Law and its Implications, by Madeleine Colvin

1989

January 24: Strategy for the 1990s launched under the new name Liberty at press conference held at the Institute of Contemporary Arts in London. Membership increased by 1700 (20 per cent) in first three months of 1989.

April: AGM supports need for legislation to control extreme forms of pornography, in continuing debate over question of censorship (eventually resolved at the 1991 AGM)

Summer: Sarah Spencer resigns as General Secretary – succeeded by Andrew Puddephatt.

Publications
Women Inside: the Experience of Women Remand Prisoners in Holloway, by Silvia Casale (Civil Liberties Trust)

The Gibraltar Report, by Hilary Kitchen
Decade of Decline: Civil Liberties in the Thatcher Years, by Peter Thornton QC
Right of Silence: the Case for Retention, by James Woods and Adam Crawford
(Civil Liberties Trust)

1990

May: Harriet Harman (former Legal Officer) and Patricia Hewitt (former General Secretary) win case in European Court against the British Government over surveillance by MI5 whilst working for NCCL.

Financial crisis – staffing levels reduced from 16 to 14.5.

Publications

The Economic League: the silent McCarthyism, by Mark Hollingsworth and Charles Tremayne
Application Refused, by Ian Linn (Civil Liberties Trust)
In Defence of the Realm, by Richard Norton-Taylor (Civil Liberties Trust)
1992 and All That, by Michael Spencer (Civil Liberties Trust)

1991

January: 'Civil liberties in time of war' campaign launched during Gulf War – support for rights of Middle Eastern nationals detained without trial.

October: Own Bill of Rights published as part of Bill of Rights Campaign.

Campaign launched for changes in the Criminal Justice system, focusing particularly on cases of miscarriages of justice.

Civil Liberty re-named *Civil Liberty Agenda.*

Publications

A People's Charter – Liberty's Bill of Rights

1992

February: Miscarriage of Justice network launched

April: Northern Ireland Human Rights Assembly convened.

November 11: Justice Day – part of the Criminal Justice Campaign.

Publications

Unequal Before the Law: Sentencing in Magistrates' Courts in England and Wales, by A Wynne and P Priestley

1993

June: Liberty and over 20 other groups launch two-year campaign to highlight British Government's human rights record. First report, produced jointly with MIND, is *People with Mental Health Problems and Learning Disability*.

July: Runciman Report published, followed by publication of second of Liberty's Human Rights Convention reports (on Criminal Justice) and presentation by Andrew Puddephatt of a petition with over 15000 signatures to the Home Office.

November 13: 'Talking Liberties' Conference attracts over 500 people to discuss a variety of human rights themes.

December: Criminal Justice and Public Order Bill proposes, amongst other things, abolition of right of silence of accused persons.

Publications
Broken Covenants (Northern Ireland Human Rights Assembly report)
People with Mental Health Problems and Learning Disability
Criminal Justice and Civil and Political Liberties
Racism: the Destruction of Civil and Political Liberties

1994

January 11: Launch of 'pro-bono' panel of City solicitors firms prepared to take on certain civil liberties cases for free.

February: Writing for Liberty event at the Institute of Contemporary Arts in which over 20 leading writers make public readings from their own work.

March: Continued opposition to Criminal Justice Bill. Campaign against proposed abolition of right of silence. Briefing for members of House of Lords held in conjunction with Justice and Charter 88.

Issue briefings about other aspects of the Bill – restrictions on the rights of travellers, increased police powers, restrictions to the right of peaceful protest, threats to the lifestyles of ravers and squatters.

Membership stands at 5,250 individuals, with 425 affiliated groups.

Publications
Democracy and Human Rights in the UK
Women's Rights, Human Rights
Sexuality and the State

Appendix 2: Major office holders

General Secretary

Ronald Kidd 1934-1941

Nancy Bell (Acting). 1941 (3 months only)

Elizabeth Acland Allen . . . . 1941-1960 (latterly Hon. Secretary)

Martin Ennals 1960-1966

Tony Smythe 1966-1972

Martin Loney . . . . January 1973-June 1974

Patricia Hewitt 1974-1983

Sarah Spencer (Acting) . . . . June-December 1983

Larry Gostin 1983-May 1985

Sarah Spencer (Acting) . . . . May-June 1985

Sarah Spencer. . . . . July 1985-1989

Marie Staunton

(Acting, during Sarah Spencer's absence on maternity leave) . . . 1986

Andrew Puddephatt . . . . 1989-to date

Director

Ronald Kidd . . . . November 1941-March 1942

President

EM Forster 1934-1936

Henry Nevinson 1936-1941

EM Forster 1942

Malcolm B Purdie 1966-1973

Select Bibliography

Original sources:

Brynmor Jones Library, University of Hull: archive of the National Council for Civil Liberties, reference DCL

Public Record Office, Kew, London: records of the Metropolitan Police, reference MEPO

The Council's journals:

Free Speech & Assembly Bulletin 1934-1937

News Sheet 1935-1937

Civil Liberty 1937-1975 (also doubled as *Annual Report* in some years)

Rights 1976-1984

Civil Liberty 1985-1990

Civil Liberty Agenda 1991-to date

Other publications:

Anderson, Gerald D, *Fascists, Communists, and the National Government: Civil Liberties in Great Britain 1931-1937* (Columbia & London, University of Missouri Press, 1983)

Benewick, Robert, 'British pressure group politics: the National Council for Civil Liberties', *Annals of the American Academy of Political & Social Science*, May 1974, pp.145-157

Cockburn, Claud, 'Civil liberties', *Punch*, 23 Feb.1955, pp.262-265

Cox, Barry, *Civil Liberties in Britain* (Harmondsworth, Penguin, 1975)

Furbank, PN, *EM Forster: a life*, vol.2 (London, Secker & Warburg, 1978)

Gostin, Larry, ed., *Civil Liberties in Conflict* (London, Routledge, 1988)

Hewitt, Patricia, *The Abuse of Power: Civil Liberties in the United Kingdom* (Oxford, Martin Robertson, 1982)

Kidd, Ronald, *British Liberty in Danger: an introduction to the study of civil rights* (London, Lawrence & Wishart, 1940)

Lilly, Mark, *The National Council for Civil Liberties: the first fifty years* (London, Macmillan, 1984)

Martin, Kingsley, *Editor: a second volume of autobiography, 1931-45* (London, Hutchinson, 1968)

Pritt, DN, *Autobiography. Volume 2: Brass Hats and Bureaucrats* (London, Lawrence & Wishart, 1966)

Scaffardi, Sylvia, *Fire Under the Carpet: Working for Civil Liberties in the Thirties* (London, Lawrence & Wishart, 1986)

Stammers, Neil, *Civil Liberties in Britain During the 2nd World War* (London, Croom Helm, 1983)

Thornton, Peter, *Decade of Decline: Civil Liberties in the Thatcher Years* (London, NCCL, 1989)

Wallington, Peter, ed., *Civil Liberties in 1984* (Oxford, Robertson, 1984)

Index

Langdon-Davies, BN 2
Lansbury, George 6, 23
Larkin, Philip ix
Laski, Professor Harold 5-6, 12, 16,
    26-27
Law and Liberty League 1
law-breaking 30
League of Nations Union 18
Lee, Heaton 30
Lehmann, Beatrix 23
Lennon, Kenneth 48
lesbian and gay rights 49-50, 61
Lewis Committee (on courts martial
    procedures) 31
lie detectors 54
Lindop Committee (on Data
    Protection) 50
local government 51
London County Council
    elections (1937) 19
London Provincial Films Motor
    Transport Company Ltd 7
London Trades Council 9, 18
Londonderry shootings (1972) 48
Loney, Martin 47, 49
Low, David 6, 10
Lubbock, Eric (Lord
    Avebury) 43-44, 48, 53

MacDonald, Ramsay 6
McGrath, John 36
McKay, RG 12
McKeag, William 11
magistrates, bias of (Harworth Colliery
    dispute) 17-18
Mallalieu, Ann 62
Mallalieu, EL 11
Malleson, Miles 10
Mallon, Dr JJ 23
Manchester Free Trade Hall 13
Manchester Guardian 5-6
Mann, Tom 4
married women, rights of 48, 52
Martin Ennals Human Rights Award 63
Martin, Kingsley 3-7, 10, 20, 27-28, 30
Massingham, HW 2
Mayhew, John 45-46
Mellish, Robert 36
Mental Deficiency Act (1913) 33-35
mental health 33-35, 53, 61

Mental Health Act (1959) 35
Mental Health (Amendment)
    Act (1982) 53
Mental Health Review Tribunals 35
Metropolitan Police 24
    Commissioner of the 3, 16, 24
MI5 24-25, 64
Miliband, Ralph 45
Milne, AA 6
MIND (National Association for Mental
    Health) 61
miners' dispute
    at Harworth (1936-37) 16-18
    national strike (1984-85) 54-56
    NCCL inquiries 17-18, 55-56
Mineworkers' Federation of Great
    Britain 18
miscarriages of justice
    Birmingham Six 62
    Challenor Case 43
    John McGrath 36
    Miscarriage of Justice Network 62
    Timothy Evans 36
Mitford, Jessica 40
Morris, William 1
Morrison, Herbert 29
Mosley, Sir Oswald 13-14, 19, 29
musicians and artists banned by the
    BBC 22-23

National Association for Mental Health
    (MIND) 61
National Council Against Conscription 1
National Council for Civil Liberties
    (World War One) 1-2
National Computing Centre 44
National Council of Labour 25
National Front 51, 54-55
National Unemployed Workers'
    Movement 2, 4, 12
National Union of Journalists 18
National Union of Mineworkers 54-56
Neuberger, Rabbi Julia 58
Nevinson, Mrs Evelyn Sharp 5
Nevinson, Henry W 4, 6, 19, 23, 25-26,
    28, 31
New Party 13
New Statesman and Nation 3, 26
News Sheet (NCCL journal) 15, 20-21
Nicolson, Harold 29